SOPER, Tony

Tony Soper's bird
table book

TONY SOPER'S
Bird Table Book

The complete guide to attracting birds
and other wildlife to your garden

Illustrated by Dan Powell

David and Charles

For David St John Thomas

A DAVID & CHARLES BOOK
Copyright © David & Charles Limited 2006

David & Charles is an F+W Publications Inc. company
4700 East Galbraith Road
Cincinnati, OH 45236

First published in the UK in 2006

Text copyright © Tony Soper 2006
Illustrations copyright © Dan Powell 2006

ISBN-13: 978-0-7153-2413-4 hardback
ISBN-10: 0-7153-2413-6 hardback

Printed in China by RR Donnelley
for David & Charles
Brunel House   Newton Abbot   Devon

Head of Publishing	Ali Myer
Commissioning Editor	Mic Cady
Editor	Ame Verso
Project Editor	Sylvia Sullivan
Art Editor	Mike Moule
Designer	Sarah Clark
Production Controller	Ros Napper

Visit our website at www.davidandcharles.co.uk

David & Charles books are available from all good
bookshops; alternatively you can contact our Orderline
on 0870 9908222 or write to us at FREEPOST EX2 110,
D&C Direct, Newton Abbot, TQ12 4ZZ (no stamp required
UK only); US customers call 800-289-0963 and Canadian
customers call 800-840-5220.

Contents

Foreword

The Bird Table Book, published in 1965, reappeared in several guises as The New Bird Table Book and The Bird Table Book in Colour. The first edition of BIRDS, the RSPB members' magazine, in January 1966, reported that more than 2,000 people had attended the RSPB's London Day, where a special attraction was the visit of Mr Tony Soper, and Mr Robert Gillmor, The Bird Table Book's illustrator. Sadly, there is no review of the book: details were included in a leaflet sent to all RSPB members.

This was the first book to advise how to make the garden more attractive to birds, not just with bird tables, but with innovative feeding techniques, bird nestboxes, water and all the paraphernalia now taken for granted. It stimulated the growth of many suppliers of bird food, tables and boxes – now a multi-million pound business – and helped fuel the rapid growth of the RSPB, from the 25,000 or so in 1965 towards a million.

The original jacket is decorated with a bold Gillmor linocut: a great tit about to alight on a peanut string on the front and great spotted woodpeckers feeding from a birch log, with holes filled with food, on the back. The jacket wording tells us that, 'Although faintly surprised to be asked to write a book about bird gardening, he tackled the job with characteristic enthusiasm and thoroughness. His straightforward approach reflects his strongly held conviction that animals are fellow-creatures to be enjoyed only with a civilized respect and tolerance.'

Tony's book had a distinctive lightness of touch, an almost conversational informality that most subsequent wildlife writers have found difficult to capture. It made his work immediately appealing and has continued with great distinction and style ever since. It may seem easy, but it is not.

Tony contributed a page to *BIRDS* for 50 issues. These columns, unfailingly produced on time, often emailed from some distant ocean, fitting exactly to space every time, always hit the mark with his readers, who enjoyed his personal take on issues of the day combined with stories of the birds in his garden, or on his travels around the world.

Tony was best known as a film maker in 1965, having graduated from studio manager to features producer at the BBC, where he helped to create the famous Natural History Unit with Desmond Hawkins. He has made many scores of television appearances, from the famous Johnny Morris *Animal Magic* series and *Animal Marvels* to *Nature*, *The Natural World*, *Discovering Animals*, *Wildtrack* and an intermittent series of live *Birdwatch* broadcasts from various places around the world, themselves paving the way for subsequent wildlife-watching shows.

His writing expanded, too, books about the seashore, owls and Antarctic wildlife prominent amongst his output. Always a popular and frequent presenter of talks and films at public events, in recent years Tony has spent much time putting together wildlife cruises and acting as guide and celebrity attraction on ships around the world. As a qualified diver and yachtmaster, living in a house on a Devon shore, he has an affinity with the sea and its shores, delighting in paddling about a beach or operating a boat, wherever he is in the world.

He owes a lot to those peanuts in 1965 – and birds well beyond the confines of our gardens owe a lot to him.

Rob Hume
Editor
RSPB *BIRDS* magazine

Introduction

Many crumbs have been eaten by many robins since this book was first launched 40 years ago. And interest in bird gardening continues to grow, as my postman and email provider will confirm! Each new edition reflects the changing character of the bird table scene. When the first *Bird Table Book* was written, no siskin had ever taken a peanut, so far as we know. Now siskins are two-a-penny on the bird feeders, joining reed buntings and lesser spotted woodpeckers, and also ring-necked parakeets and other exotic creatures. Even little egrets threaten to invade the garden pond.

It is clear that more species are learning to take advantage of bird tables and feeding stations – just as well, when so much of their natural feeding ground is being swallowed up for unsympathetic development. All the more reason to try to create a house and garden that takes into account the requirements of wildlife as well as your own.

As I look out of my kitchen window I see a continuous stream of tits and finches coming to take advantage of the nuts and seeds on offer from a selection of cunning devices. Living on the edge of coastal Devon we even get cirl buntings coming to bathe in the bird bath. Maybe that is more than most of us can hope for, but it is still a fact that providing a range of foods, from kitchen scraps to more sophisticated commercial products, can bring surprises to your garden.

Gardening with birds in mind goes hand in hand with encouraging other wild creatures. This hummingbird hawk moth – here sipping nectar from buddleia – is so birdlike that it could be mistaken for a real hummingbird.

Gardens can be wonderfully rich in wildlife. In the scene opposite a greenfinch and a charm of goldfinches are attracted by the feeder, while the blackbird is taking the worm the hedgehog would also have enjoyed had he got there earlier.

Although the individual species that visit our gardens will vary greatly, depending on the surrounding area and local habitats, there is much that we can do to enhance our own individual patches to encourage more birds and other wildlife to visit. If they decide to stay and breed or overwinter, we feel doubly privileged. This book shows you how to ensure that your garden provides the basic requirements of food, water and shelter that all creatures need to survive. It also tells you a little about the commonest species you are likely to see and what features will attract them. Wild animals cannot be guaranteed, of course, and you may never see a kingfisher diving into your garden pond but by creating a pond you have at least made a start! It is the element of surprise that is probably the greatest draw of wildlife watching.

Feeding birds (and hedgehogs, badgers and toads, too) is a rewarding activity. Not only are these creatures good to see about the garden, but their relationships with each other, with us, and with their surroundings, are of absorbing interest. So spare them an honest crust, with a bit of cheese as well.

Tony Soper
South Devon, May 2006
www.tonysoper.com

Bird Gardening

It is not necessary to travel to faraway places in order to enjoy nature. A healthy slice of it lies on the other side of your garden window, and a not inconsiderable slice actually lives in the house with you! A town house, with a garden of window boxes, a paved yard or a roof area, may attract only a few flying insects and visiting house sparrows and pigeons. A small plot with a few bushes and trees will see an influx of blackbirds and a few tits. A larger garden with more trees, more shrubbery and a lawn will see robins and dunnocks, chaffinches, greenfinches, wrens and perhaps a hedgehog. With mature trees the woodland species come flooding in – jays, woodpigeons, more finches, treecreepers, blackcaps and thrushes, squirrels and owls. A mature garden is a haven for a host of bugs, birds and beasts. This chapter looks at making the most of the structure and planting of your own garden to maximize its wildlife potential.

Historical background

On the grand scale, management for birds involves the farming of large acreages in order to provide favourable conditions for resident or visiting species, thus increasing their numbers. The pioneers of this sort of activity worked in America, where suitable lakes and lakeside vegetation are still strictly controlled for the benefit of migratory wildfowl. In Britain, the Royal Society for Protection of Birds (RSPB) manages a network of bird reserves which, at the same time, serves the purposes of other wildlife. The productive and healthy farming of any habitat will support the liveliest population of birds, so what's good for worms is good for birds, too, in the long run.

It seems likely that Saint Cuthbert, living the simple life at his hermitage on Inner Farne, off the Northumberland coast, in the 7th century AD, ran the first bird reserve in the

St Cuthbert declared the world's first nature reserve in the 7th century, protecting 'cuddy ducks' (eiders).

world. His was an all-embracing love, encompassing otters and seals as well as eiders and gannets, to say nothing of his fellow men. He enjoyed all his birds, but had a special affection for the eiders, affording them total protection from the hunters. His idyllic group of islands is still a wildlife sanctuary, under the protection of the National Trust.

Inevitably, the earliest records of active bird management derive from their economic value. Some centuries ago pigeons were encouraged to breed in convenient coastal caves, for example at East Wemyss in Fife (although the practice originated much earlier in the Middle East), in order to take advantage of the resulting fat squabs. And while wildfowl had been hunted and herded in northern countries (during their flightless period of moult), the first account of managed breeding herds in Britain comes from Abbotsbury in Dorset. Here the monks of the Benedictine Monastery encouraged the nesting mute swans, taking a proportion of the fat cygnets for the table. The first written records of this activity were in 1393. The swans did well on the rich feeding in the coastal lagoons of the Fleet, inside the Chesil Bank. In 1543, Henry VIII granted the right to keep the herd to the Fox Strangways family, which has protected the swans through the years to the present day. The swanherd watches over a flock that numbers some four hundred to five hundred birds at breeding time, but rises to nearer one thousand in winter.

The legacy of the early bird gardeners is that we can enjoy birds, like this displaying greenfinch, from the comfort of our own home.

Early bird park

It was Squire Charles Waterton, of Walton Hall near Wakefield in Yorkshire, who deliberately set out to create a bird park of his property, and thus he probably became the proprietor of the first nature reserve in Britain to be established for pleasure and enjoyment. In 1817, he began a ten-year plan that systematically developed his 105 ha (260 acres) into a sanctuary designed to improve the prospects for birds. He banned shooting altogether, threatening to strangle his gamekeeper if he shot any barn owls, and forbade boating on his lake during the waterfowl breeding season. He also built a high wall round the entire property to exclude casual disturbance, and dogs. Foxes were trapped and deported, and even badgers were shown the door, in rather drastic moves to reduce the hazards to birds. Curiously, though, he encouraged weasels, inveterate small-bird killers, but this was because he had an obsession with ridding the estate of the abundant brown rats, the 'Hanoverian' rats, which he hated.

Waterton encouraged weasels, knowing that they were enthusiastic bird killers, because he detested rats ...

Nestbox experiments

Waterton's enclosed reserve, and his management of it, was highly successful. In a letter to his friend George Ord, dated 1849, he wrote '... my carrion crows, herons, hawks and magpies have done very well this year and I have a fine brood of kingfishers. They may thank their stars that they have my park wall to protect them. But for it their race would be extinct in this depraved and demoralized part of Yorkshire.'

He experimented with various kinds of nestbox to encourage owls (and starlings) to breed. He ensured, too, the luxuriant growth of ivy, correctly deciding that it was a beneficial plant that would provide food and shelter for birds without damaging trees. Waterton was far in advance of his contemporaries in understanding the general principles of wildlife management on an ecological basis, in spite of his aberrations. He sued the owners of a nearby soap works when he considered their effluent was polluting his lake (the law, reflecting the industrial spirit of an age, awarded him derisory damages). Interestingly, Waterton's relations with fellow workers in his field were inclined to be hot-tempered. He despised the museum workers, calling them 'closet naturalists' (at a time when taxonomy, the science of classification, was seen as the only fit pursuit for a professional), and positively gloried in field-work as well as his amateur status. When he shot birds for his collection (he was an enthusiastic taxidermist) he chose only males, because he preferred the bright colours! However, in an age when estates were kept up for the production of game, and keepers were wedded to the concept of vermin destruction, with little understanding of the relationship between species, Waterton's ideas were regarded as highly eccentric. This epithet he rejected but invited time and time again by indulging in a series of bizarre exploits (one of his many party tricks was to scratch the back of his head with the big toe of his right foot). Waterton must bear his share of responsibility for the outdated belief that naturalists were not entirely stable creatures.

By the end of his time Waterton had recorded 122 species of bird in his park, including osprey, hobby, hooded crow and crossbill. Sadly, after his death, the estate was bought by a man who 'improved' it back to conventional tidiness and ruined his life's work.

Pest control

Charles Waterton was among those responsible for the introduction of the little owl to Britain. He thought it would help to control unwelcome bugs on his land, for the little owl feeds largely on invertebrates. His attempt, in 1842, failed, but the little owl became a successful colonist after further introductions in the 1890s.

Aims of the bird gardener

Large-scale bird management tends to be connected with agriculture, or sport (in the field of game conservation). But there is plenty of potential for influencing the lives of birds so that their lot is improved and our enjoyment of their company increased. And, for this process, the term 'bird gardening' is a convenient one, whether the area in question is around a factory, a school playing-field, or the garden of a house. Man's works inevitably attract their quota of wildlife, just as inevitably as they deprive some species of their living space – they not only diminish, but provide opportunities. The bird gardener seeks to enhance these possibilities. After all, the birds will come whether we like it or not, so we might as well enjoy them. And by providing new possibilities we may reverse the trend towards impoverishment in terms of species diversity.

Quite apart from their practical usefulness as a means of pest control and as agents of seed dispersal, birds are important to us as a food source. But not only are they useful, they are beautiful as well. Their colour and movement, their calls and songs add new dimensions to existence. So the diligent bird gardener sets out to please them and to organize a welcome. Put simply, this means providing food, water and shelter.

Food as fuel

Food is the prime requirement of any animal. As fuel, it provides energy, promotes health, allows for defence capability and reproduction. Water is equally important, not just for drinking but as a requirement in the maintenance of plumage. Shelter provides protection from enemies and the elements, and serves as a nursery. A long-established, mature garden with a diversity of shrubs and flowering plants, with a mix of young, prime and decaying trees, some clad in ivy, an orchard with lichen-encrusted apple trees and surrounded by thick impenetrable hedges, allied to a house with plenty of corners and ledges, to say nothing of cracks and crevices, is already a most productive bird haven. The highest bird density in Britain is found in suburban gardens and estates, where the habitat resembles an endless woodland edge rather than the less birdy forest

Bird gardeners welcome sparrowhawks as well as house martins!

interior. But it has to be recognized that this habitat doesn't suit all species, so special attention needs to be given to those that have been dispossessed by house building. This is why the bird gardener also supports the work done by organizations like the RSPB.

In the beginning

A newly constructed house with a lot of bare earth and newly planted saplings offers little attraction for wildlife, so at this stage a well-stocked bird table and a drinking/bathing pool are important. Natural food will be scarce so make special provision. The species you see will at first depend on the kind of country that has been converted, and the surrounding habitats. If your house was built on a drained salt marsh then you may find meadow pipits coming to feed on the bird table. Mostly, though, the ecological changes wrought by the builder result in the less adaptable species disappearing, trying their luck elsewhere. New development will be unattractive for specialist and finicky creatures like stone-curlews, wheatears, Dartford warblers, bearded tits and snipe – all animals which require open space and don't take kindly to disruption of their hunting lands.

Long-tailed tits patrol and explore gardens in cheerful parties. These youngsters are under orders to sit tight.

But while heath and marshland species are ill served by built development, woodland and some water-loving species can find gardens to be an acceptable substitute for their original habitat. When ecological succession – and a certain amount of management – provides mature trees, some decaying timber, creeper-clad walls and an abundance of shrubbery and secret places, then the animal population will show a distinct improvement. Plenty of light, shady corners, trees, shrubs and grassy glades; plenty of natural food and shelter; bird-table scraps and gadgets; a grassy lawn and a pond – all this adds up to good news for birds and for mammals like squirrels, foxes, hedgehogs and moles. Small birds are happy and flourish and, if you have a decent-sized lawn, you'll also find magpies, rooks, jackdaws, gulls, starlings and pigeons.

New roots

If you are faced with the prospect of a newly built house, surrounded by a morass of subsoil, you must obviously survey the situation carefully before rushing into a planting programme. First of all, make sure that your precious topsoil is carefully replaced. Ensure, also, that any existing boundary walls or hedges, and other features such as trees, ponds or wells, are carefully preserved, so that you are able to write them into your plan. Determine the soil type, consider the orientation of the ground, and cast a long look at the biological opportunities that abut on to your property. While your neighbours may jealously guard their territorial rights, wilder animals will use the highways that suit their purposes without any consideration for property law. The object is to reinforce the positive advantages of your own patch,to introduce complementary possibilities, and to

exert what influence you can on the
neighbouring land. If there is a public park
nearby, for instance, it may be worth encouraging
the authorities to improve their tree-planting plans
by concentrating on native trees, thus discouraging
dark and dismal laurel or rhododendron plantations.

   In the garden, the object should be to plant for maximum nut,
berry, seed and insect production, to provide a measure of cover, and
to provide water. In a newly planted garden, which will inevitably lack abundant
bird food, a bird table will be most important, but the long-term plan should be
to provide as varied and plentiful a mix of natural food as possible. Make the place
an adventure course for enterprising bird explorers – a varied terrain of lawns, rockeries,
walls, miniature hills, valleys, streams and ponds. If the visiting birds find a cornucopia,
they are more likely to move in and settle.

Good neighbours

The process starts with an abundance of greenery, providing food for insects which in
turn support the blue tits, which in their turn support sparrowhawks. The very nature
of gardening itself, the process of turning soil and planting new life, encourages a
particular group of birds – those which are best able to adapt to our activities. Robins,
thrushes, house sparrows, starlings and dunnocks are all predisposed to live alongside
us and will soon take advantage of new housing potential. On the other hand, many
of our summer visitors, such as warblers, need to be encouraged, by providing a wealth
of foliage and flowers that support quantities of insects.

A variety of weeds

Seriously consider the possibility of keeping a wilderness area in part of your garden, a wild jungle of weeds and shrubs which can be visited by hunting bands of itinerant finches. If you can bring yourself to face the neighbours, have a nettle bed. Young fresh nettles are good to eat, ask any caterpillar. But stir yourself to cutting portions of the bed every now and then, to keep those fresh young shoots coming right through the season. A clump of nettles will be a hothouse breeding-ground for insects and spiders, and the leaves will serve as egg-laying sites for butterflies. If possible, the wilderness area should have a dark and secret roosting-place where birds may rest and recuperate, but the most important factor is a flourishing variety of seed-producing 'weeds'.

Enjoy your weeds

Nettles are good value – and beautiful, too. Other useful plants from a wildlife point of view are knapweed, teasel, groundsel, chickweed and dandelion. Although these sound like a veritable catalogue of disaster, the advantage of these native plants is that they offer first-class feeding opportunities to birds that are well equipped to exploit them. Goldfinches, for example, use their long probing bills to extract the seeds from prickly thistle and teasel heads. It is true that wild thistles have an unfortunate tendency to run riot, but the ornamental varieties, which are more restrained territorially, still produce plenty of seeds. Cow parsley, that vigorous and glorious hedgerow edge plant, should be a welcome member of the wilderness community, and greenfinches much enjoy its seeds. The same is true of fat hen, a plant cordially disliked by 'real' gardeners but equally cordially enjoyed by finches when they go for the seeds in late summer.

Bramble should find a place somewhere. Apart from providing good roosting and nesting potential, its flowers support insects, comma caterpillars feed on its leaves and, in due course, thrushes and blackbirds take the berries, voiding the pips which in their turn are found by passing finches.

Butterflies find nettles perfect as a home for their eggs; these emerging peacock caterpillars dine on the leaves. And remember the old rhyme if you are stung ... 'Nettle in, dock out, dock rub nettle out'!

Trees and shrubs

Obviously, your ability to nurture trees will depend on the size of your plot, and it is true that plenty of low, dense cover is far more important in a small garden. If you can possibly find room for it, grow one tall tree – for instance a poplar – that will serve as a song post for a thrush. But even if denied a natural song perch, your thrush or blackbird will happily accept the second-best option of a chimney pot or television aerial. And if you are lucky enough to have an old decaying tree on your patch, then cherish it.

A 'charm' of goldfinches uses sharply pointed bills to extract the seeds from prickly thistle and teasel heads.

The benefits of death

Dead trees may be a forester's nightmare, but for a garden-naturalist the best thing of all is for a tree to die of old age, perhaps hastened by wood-boring beetles and a fungus that sucks the life out of it. This is as it should be, for a garden without decaying wood is impoverished. A vast community of plants, fungi and animals live on dead wood and help with the rotting process of recycling. Death and decay are a necessary and healthy part of life. This is especially true in a forest, for where a tree topples, the leafy canopy is broken and a pool of sunlight penetrates the floor. The light stimulates saplings to grow and race each other towards the sky where daylight is unlimited. In time the open wound in the canopy is healed. Again, it is the sunlight which makes the whole system work. Every blade of grass and every leaf is a chemical factory soaking up sunlight and ultimately providing energy-rich substances from which flowers, fruits and timber are made. Nutrients in dead timber and leaves are essential to the continuing story. Consider making a log pile somewhere in a corner. A gathering of logs will provide shelter for an astonishing number of creatures. In the cool, damp, secret place under the logs there will be slugs and snails, centipedes, beetles, ants and spiders, to say nothing of frogs, toads and newts if you have a pond nearby. Even a hedgehog may come to make a home. Felling should be regarded only as a last resort, in cases of

Wrens are great insect-hunters, but will also search for spiders. This one is working a log pile.

potential danger. Enjoy the well-grown trees you have; plant new ones for your children and grandchildren.

Where you have space to plant new trees, choose native species by preference rather than the exotics which nurserymen will be only too glad to recommend. The foliage, fruits and seeds of native trees will be more efficiently harvested by our birds, which are programmed by long experience to utilize them to best advantage. Be careful to consider their eventual size when you are planting specimens that seem puny at the time. So allow space, but allow for thinning.

Use natives

Our native trees are better able to withstand our moist and wayward weather, and harmonize well with the other plants and animals in their community. Mature oaks and limes support a flourishing community of their own, but of course they do take time to grow. 'Two hundred years a-growing, two hundred a-thinking and two hundred a-dying' just about sums up an oak's life, but for all that people think of it in terms of slow growth, it can reach a good girth and height well within one man's lifetime. In forest conditions an oak may reach up 40m (100ft), but a lime may exceed that by yet another 9m (30ft). The lime, however, is very amenable to pruning. One of the few forest trees to be pollinated by insects, it hums with activity in summer. One particular species of aphid enjoys the sap of limes, whose sweet sticky honeydew attracts queues of bees and other insects. So naturally the lime tree is a favourite with birds, which also enjoy its autumn fruits.

If you are looking for trees that will grow fast and provide a quick return for garden birds, choose ash, elm, birch, willow and native cherry. Ash grows rapidly in any soil, and its seeds – keys – are an important food source for bullfinches and others. Birch, too, will grow fast in most soils, but it is somewhat disease-prone, an advantage perhaps for the bird gardener who lives in the hope of providing woodpeckers with an easily drilled home. Its seeds are eagerly taken by redpolls, siskins and tits. For smaller gardens there is a dwarf version, *Betula pendula youngii*, a weeping birch.

The purple berries of elder are enjoyed by dozens of species of birds, so it clearly merits a place in any birdman's garden. The native form is preferable to cultivars; it grows fast, almost anywhere, and it is hardy, taking plenty of punishment. Since its leaves appear early in the season it provides valuable nesting cover for our native songbirds, which breed earlier than the migrant visitors.

Learn to love decay

Ideally, trees in a garden should exhibit a mixed age structure, with young trees to allow plenty of light to reach the ground plants, and prime trees to provide an abundance of food and shelter. In the long run, decaying trees are the most valuable of all, allowing living space and providing sustenance to the greatest variety and number of insects and plants which live off their bounty. If you find the spectacle of a slowly dying tree a trifle uncomfortable, encourage it with ivy or clematis or honeysuckle to make it look more interesting!

Fruit trees

Fruit trees in an orchard supply large quantities of bird food, both in terms of insects and, more controversially, the fruit itself. But it may be possible to leave some of the fruit on a few of the trees, so that it will decay gently into the kind of soft flesh for which thrushes are so grateful in the winter. In summer, blue tits will hunt over apple trees and take quantities of the codling moth caterpillars that cause so much damage. Both apples and pears suit birds very well, as do most other fruits. Wild cherry is a satisfactory bird tree, but avoid the sterile double-flowered cultivated varieties. Blackbirds and starlings, too, will be pleased to help you harvest redcurrant and flowering

Elderberries are much appreciated by birds, including this starling. A flock of starlings can strip a tree of its berries in no time at all.

Jays hoard acorns for a rainy day, not all get eaten, some become mighty oaks.

currants. Of course, it is easy to object to the way birds take their tithe of fruit and table vegetables, but the other side of the coin is a valid one: starlings, for instance, if you are lucky enough to have any, eat large numbers of leatherjackets.

Red berries

Spindle is a useful shrub, growing as much as 4.6m (15ft) high. Bushy and ornamental, it prefers chalky or lime-rich soil. In autumn it sports attractive colours, after producing a rich crop of pink and orange fruit. However, this fruit is poisonous to humans and should not be planted if you have young children. Rowan (mountain ash) is another first-class bird tree; it needs plenty of light but is not fussy, although it prefers a light soil. Fruiting in August, its brilliant coral-red berries are a magnet for mistle thrushes, blackbirds, song thrushes and starlings, which will strip the tree long before winter. A useful bonus with rowan is that it will provide protection for your property against the evil designs of any passing witch. And if the extensive rowan berry crops of Scandinavia fail, then in winter eastern Britain sometimes enjoys an invasion of the spectacular waxwings, birds which depend upon the berries and hunt rather desperately through our hedgerows in search of substitutes.

Hedges are very important to birds, providing endless opportunities for both food and shelter. So it is worth spending some time and effort on growing satisfactory ones. If possible, the ideal is to mix the plants so that they provide a range of food choices, which peak at different times of the year. Hawthorn, for example, makes a good basic choice. As a free-growing tree it will grow quite tall, but it bows gracefully to life as a disciplined hedge – cut to shape, layered and trimmed, it provides dense cover. It grows quickly, almost anywhere, and its spiny branches soon form an excellent protective barrier. It presents lovely colour in spring, while its secret interior houses songbirds' nests. From

August it provides a generous crop of scarlet haws, luscious berries, which are taken by thrushes and blackbirds, as well as winter visitors like fieldfares and redwings, to say nothing of waxwings. Be careful not to confuse hawthorn with blackthorn, whose sloes are not so popular with birds.

Holly is another first-class hedge plant, although it is reluctant to fruit when it is hard clipped, and it prefers well-drained soil. It may be a slow grower, so make a point of buying vigorous (and expensive) stock from the nurserymen. If you are free-growing it for berries, make sure you plant females, but there must be one pollinating male nearby to be sure of effective fertilization. The cultivated forms are most reliable. 'Golden King' (a female) grows to 3m (10ft) and crops well; 'Madame Briot' to 5.5m (18ft), produces golden berries. As a hedge plant, holly mixes well, providing a good evergreen cat-proof hedge with an impenetrable roosting and nesting fastness. Birds are not enthusiastic about the berries, except in hard weather, but the holly hedge pays its way by virtue of its secure winter roosting potential.

Versatile hazel

Hazel is a useful addition to the hedgerow, on the grounds of diversity, in that it provides a welcome nut harvest in August and September. It flourishes best on rich, chalky soils which are not too wet. Find a sunny space or two for some crab-apple trees in the hedge, as they are an invaluable source of winter food for thrushes in hard weather. Fieldfares and redwings will enjoy the flesh, leaving the pips for finches. The fruit generally resembles outsize yellow cherries and is reluctant to fall, even after the leaves have been shed, thus providing good food very late in the winter. There are various ornamental versions but it is probably best to stick to the native wild crab-apple *Malus pumila*, though an ornamental variety 'Gold Hornet' has been recommended for its abundant crop of small yellow fruits, much appreciated by thrushes.

When the rowan berry crops of Scandinavia fail, these showy waxwings become welcome winter visitors to Britain, and often turn up in supermarket car parks.

Siskins and redpolls often keep company in winter, here amongst alder, a species currently suffering from a severe fungal disease.

Tits work hard to get at the pips, and chaffinches take the pips after the fruits have been hacked open by thrushes. The variety 'Veitches Scarlet' produces large, scarlet fruits.

Yew is another useful hedgerow plant. It will suffer endless clipping and live a long and fruitful life as a 1.8m (6ft) bush, though if left untouched it can grow to 27.5m (90ft) and live for a thousand years. The foliage and bark, as well as the seeds, are poisonous to domestic stock so it is not suitable for farm hedges. However, it serves well in a bird garden. The evergreen hedge provides useful nest-sites and the fleshy red berries of the female tree provide good feeding for thrushes and starlings, which eat the pulp and pass on the poisonous seed without harm. Remember, incidentally, to introduce males into the hedge, though in some instances both male and female flowers appear on the same tree. Of course, a close-clipped hedge plant will not fruit as generously as a free-growing tree, but a well-varied boundary of evergreen and deciduous shrubs, together with nut-bearing plants, is a decided advantage from the birds' point of view. Do your hedging and ditching, tree lopping and any necessary felling early in the year, certainly by the end of March, and then the birds will not be disturbed at nesting time.

Bird trees for the garden

Trees are the largest features in a garden, both in terms of height and the spread of their branches and roots. In an established garden you will probably want to work with what you've already got. In a new garden the planting of trees demands considerable and careful thought, for they will dictate the basic design of your garden, influencing what can be grown near them, and the amount of light filtering down. As trees will live for many years and are difficult and costly to move when mature, make your decisions with thought for the future.

TREES FOR WILDLIFE

FOREST GIANTS
Don't plant these unless you have a giant garden!

Ash *Fraxinus excelsior* 24.4m (80ft). Popular look-out and song posts. Ash keys provide winter food, especially for bullfinches.

Beech *Fagus sylvatica* 30.5m (100ft). Beech mast is the major winter food for many garden birds. Massive form and total shade.

Oak *Quercus robur*, *Q. petraea* 24.4m (80ft). Single most important wildlife tree – fruits and insects for feeding, abundant nest sites. Huge spreading form.

Hornbeam *Carpinus betulu* 24.4m (80 ft). Greenfinches and hawfinches love winter seeds. Unfortunately hawfinches prefer trees in growing in groups, rather than single specimens.

NATIVE EVERGREENS

Holly *Ilex aquifolium* 15.2m (50ft). An important tree – nest sites, roosting, insect food and mid-winter berries. Berries only on female trees; male tree needed for pollination.

Scots pine *Pinus sylvestris* 24.4m (80ft). Too tall for most gardens. Good for corvid nests; owls, ospreys! Rich insect fauna; pine cones for crossbills.

Juniper *Juniperus communis* 4.6m (15ft). Good native with popular berries for birds and good nesting shelter. Innumerable varieties now available, choose to suit needs, but ensure it will have berries.

NON-NATIVE EVERGREENS
Speedy short-term shelter

Lawson cypress *Chamaecyparis lawsoniana* 18.3m (60ft). Tightly columnar. Many varieties: *'Elwoodii'* (bluish) is good for small gardens. Nesting for dunnock, thrushes, goldfinch. Good roosting and pinnacle song post for chaffinch and greenfinch.

Leyland cypress *Cupressocyparis leylandii* 15.2m (50ft). Fastest growing bar none. Dense foliage makes valuable shelter-belt and provides nest sites. Good wind-proof hedge protecting new plants from drying out; cut to height. Don't let it get out of hand.

DECIDUOUS NATIVES
Not giants, but nevertheless substantial

Alder *Alnus glutinosa* 18.3m (60ft). Wet sites. Insect-rich, and woodpeckers, tits, treecreepers, warblers, redpolls, siskins and others feed on winter seed cones.

Aspen *Populus tremula* 21.3m (70ft). Quick-growing, insect-rich – suits warblers and tits especially. Light shade; attractive trembling leaves.

Birch *Betula pendula*, *B. pubescens* 18.3m (60ft). Another 'top drawer' bird tree: rich in insects and seeds. Redpolls and others feed on spring catkins. Woodpeckers and willow tits nest in decaying stumps. Quick-growing; light shade.

Elder *Sambucus nigra* 6m (20ft). Not often considered for planting but a good wildlife tree. Flowers attract many insects, birds love autumn elderberries. Flowers and berries are winemaker's delight!

Hazel *Corylus avellana* 6m (20ft). Hazel nuts are important winter food for birds and mammals. Another insect-rich tree: good bird feeding.

Hawthorn *Crataegus monogyna*, *C. oxycanthoides* 6m (20ft). Intruder-deterrent hedgerow plant but also makes a good standard. A key bird tree for all-year insects and winter berries. Much used for thorny nest sites.

Larch *Larix decidua* 24.4m (80ft). Use for quick-growing shelter on a bare site. Good seed producer.

Rowan and **Whitebeam** *Sorbus aucuparia*, *S. aria* 15.2m (50ft). Attractive white flowers, light shade, heavy autumn berry crop. Quick-growing; both produce berries early in life. Added value in that it protects your property from the evil eye!

Wild cherry *Prunus avium* 21.3m (70ft). Grows to very big tree. Good nest sites; popular summer fruit crop for birds.

Willows *Salix* spp. Many species – heights vary; all first class for birds. Avoid larger species – pussy willow, *Salix caprea*, has everything to commend it – size, shape, amenable to pruning, earliest flowers, and masses of seed in autumn. Warblers, tits, goldcrests make a beeline for it and its abundance of insects.

Climbing plants

Trees, whether they are free-standing or part of a hedge system, may be much improved by teaming them with climbing plants. And if considerations of space, or respect for your neighbour's view, mean that you cannot have trees at all, then at least erect some trellis or fencing to provide something for a climber to conquer.

Honeysuckle is a liana which will entwine and climb, providing a colourful display of early flowers and heady fragrance, but in the process will allow for some secret nest-places. Its nectar is attractive to privet hawk-moths, which reach it with long probosci; blackbirds, tits and blackcaps are not enthusiastic but will take the berries. *Lonicera fragrantissima* grows bushy and is suitable as a sunny hedgerow plant; *L. periclymenum*, the native woodbine, is the entwiner and prefers some shade.

Celebrate ivy

The much-maligned ivy *Hedera helix* should be regarded with respect and cherished in any bird lover's garden. Castigated by the ignorant as a strangler of trees, it in fact does no harm except in the very rare cases when it completely covers the crown and cuts off light to the foliage. The fact is that ivy is a top-class birdman's plant. Thriving even in poor soil, it will carpet the ground till it finds an opportunity to climb. The dense, leathery leaves do not have the fragile beauty of any number of exotic imports, instead they are a robust part of the British garden and woodland scene. Climbing by virtue of the deceptively root-like hairs on its stem, ivy flowers when it reaches light. Flowering late, in September and October, it offers rich nectar at a time when this scarce commodity is particularly appreciated by butterflies, bees and other insects. Similarly, ivy fruits exceptionally late, in March and April, when its berries supply desperately needed food for wood pigeons and thrushes, to say nothing of a number of small mammals. Aside from this virtue, which should guarantee ivy a welcome in every garden, its convolutions and evergreen secret places provide a rich source of nest sites and roosting places. Through

Ivy fruits in early spring, when its berries are eagerly taken by wood pigeons.

the year, its hairy stems and
nourishing leaves support
quantities of insects, which in turn
provide food for hunting wrens and
tits. The 'Irish Ivy' *H. hibernica* is a
good cover for north-facing walls.
A rampant grower, it is dense and
grows out from the walls in bush
shapes, providing not only exceptionally
good roosting places but free thermal
insulation for the house as well.

Plants for roosting and shelter

Apart from food, one of the important bird functions
of greenery in a garden is to provide roosting shelter at
night, especially in winter when evergreens come into their own.
So, it is worth making sure that you have a fair proportion of other
evergreens, as well as ivy, in your garden, for instance in the boundary
hedge. Even laurels and rhododendrons are useful in this respect.
Town councils like them because they shade the ground and inhibit
the growth of weeds, but they nurture few insects and offer little food
value. Both common and white spruce make useful roost trees and
offer good nest-sites as well. If you are lucky enough to have a
Wellingtonia (and if you plant one remember it grows to be the biggest
tree in the world – in its native California it is known modestly as the
'Big Tree'), cherish it as the preferred roost tree for treecreepers. They
excavate an egg-shaped burrow in the spongy fibrous bark, then repair
to it for the night, tucking themselves into the hollow in a vertical
posture, bill resting on the bark and tail down, feathers fluffed out
boldly – a most astonishing sight. *Wellingtonia* was introduced to
Britain in 1853 (the year after the Duke of Wellington died). Before
this time treecreepers made hollows in rotting trees, or utilized natural
cavities or crevices behind loose bark, as of course large numbers of
them still do. But it is relatively easy to discover them on *Wellingtonia*,
sometimes as many as a dozen or so, low down on the same tree.
Leyland cypress *Cupressocyparis leylandii*, for all that it is much derided,
has great value in a bird garden for the dense shelter it provides for
roosting and nest sites.

*Treecreepers shuffle
about over tree trunks
like mice, hunting
insects and spiders.
Sometimes they will
roost (often on
Wellingtonia) in
small numbers.*

DECIDUOUS AND EVERGREEN SHRUBS AND CLIMBERS

Various forms of *Cotoneaster* are useful, as ground-huggers, bushes and climbers, because they are insect-rich as well as providing a cornucopia of berries. *C. interifolius* fruits conveniently late, between the hawthorn and ivy harvests. Thrushes, finches and tits enjoy its rich berries and it grows almost anywhere. Blackbirds are the most enthusiastic *Cotoneaster* customers. Between them, the various species provide berries from late summer through to spring. Useful cultivated forms include:

C. simonsii. Effective hedge plant, produces good bird berries. Height to 3.6m.

C. horizontalis. Deciduous. Fan-shaped cover for wall. Height up to 3m if against wall. Red berries last well into winter, especially if it grows within the territory of a blackbird, which will husband the crop and deny it to other birds.

C. 'Cornubia'. Height and spread 1.8m to 4.6m (6ft to 25ft). Deciduous. Clusters of red berries on arching branches.

C. conspicus. Sometimes known as *decorus*. Grows 1.2m to 1.8m (4ft to 6ft). Green foliage and orange berries.

C. dammeri and *C. prostratus*. Small, ground-hugging, ever spreading trailers. Good ground cover encouraging bugs.

C. franchetii. Evergreen wall climber, to 3m (10ft).

C. lacteus. Evergreen wall climber to 4.6m (25ft).

C. purpurascens. Slowly grows to small tree.

C. watereri. Slowly grows to small tree.

Like *Cotoneaster* the barberry also shows itself in a bewildering variety of forms – full species and hybrids. But all of them offer rich pickings for birds, as well as colourful foliage, which provides thick ground cover inhibiting weed growth. *Berberis vulgaris*, the common barberry, is a deciduous plant, branching thickly and growing to 1.8m (6ft), providing weed-free ground underneath. It is easy to grow, and can tolerate sun or shade – indeed, almost anything the British climate offers. Not soil-fussy, it is easily propagated from hardwood cuttings in September. Its coral red berries have a high vitamin C content and are eaten by most birds, especially blackbirds, which make a charming picture in late autumn when they perch among the fruits. Useful cultivated forms include:

B. darwinii. Evergreen, reaching and spreading to 3m (10ft). Good prickly hedge, needing only light trimming to shape. Purple/blue berries. This species hails from Chile; its berries are much enjoyed in midsummer. Recommended varieties are 'Gold' and 'Flame'.

B. aggregata. 'Buccaneer'. Deciduous. Long-lasting berries. Reaching and spreading to 2.7m (9ft).

B. wilsoniae. Deciduous. Formidable thorns make it a useful hedge plant. Translucent coral berries.

B. calliantha. Black fruits.

B. thunbergii. Height 1.8m (6ft) spread 2.4m (8ft). Berries and autumn foliage brilliant red.

The firethorn *Pyracantha coccinea* is a high-intensity, evergreen berry producer, much enjoyed by thrushes. It climbs well, fruiting even on a dark north wall, producing deep red berries and growing to 4.6m (15ft). This species hails from southern Europe. Its fruit first ripens towards the end of August but may still be available as late as mid-winter if it has been defended by a fiercely territorial blackbird. *P. atalantioides* grows to much the same height, but will take pruning and provides good nest opportunities.

If you can get it, *Coriaria xanthocarpa* is a useful suckering sub-shrub that grows slowly to provide a good ground cover over several square yards. Its foot-long racemes bear translucent yellow fruit which is much appreciated by songbirds.

Leaf litter

The leaf litter that collects under hedgebanks and shrubberies is a prime hunting ground for birds. It is a home for snails and slugs, woodlice, many insects and spiders. This sort of scrub country is very good for birds, and without it you'll never achieve a high population density. This is where you will hear the blackbird shuffling about, sorting through the debris, making a remarkable volume of noise. And the dunnock will be here, too; typically a hedge bird it is unfortunately often called a hedge sparrow. Brown it may be, but with its thin beak and plump build it's no sparrow, in form or behaviour. An unobtrusive bird, it maintains a low profile in the garden. It likes a bit of jungle, and has flourished in the garden habitat. Weed seeds in winter, insects in summer, and the birdtable when it gets the opportunity – that's the life of the dunnock, and many other birds too.

Leaf litter offers a prime hunting ground for blackbirds, which make an astonishing amount of noise as they sort through it for bugs.

Colour preference

The orange-fruited versions of firethorn seem to be preferred to the red ones, for instance. And birds seem to go for the black rather than the red berries. But it may be that the colour contrast between fruits and foliage is a factor and the degree of shininess in the fruits may also be significant. A cockshy list of preferences seems to indicate that red or crimson fruits are prime favourites, followed closely by orange and yellow. Then comes the less favoured – white, blue, brown-purple and rose-pink. Much the same is true in the case of flower colours, with the same top preferences, reds to yellows, followed by the blues and whites. House sparrows tend to attack red and yellow flowers in spring and autumn in order to eat buds and petals. In their defence, it has to be said that they enrich the soil with droppings which contain nitrogen, phosphate and lime. Like blue tits, house sparrows also enjoy nectar, and so visit clumps of red hot poker *Kniphofia uvaria*.

Red and yellow flowers are the most attractive and most frequented by birds. In this case a blue tit seeks the nectar of a red-hot poker.

Border plants

Many of the cultivated border plants provide good feeding for birds, mostly in terms of the provision of seeds. Sunflowers, for example, when left to seed, are heavy with an oil-rich bounty which is irresistible to tits, nuthatches and finches. Finches are seed specialists with sophisticated tastes, visiting plants as they come into production. Other plants produce pollen, nectar, flowers and vegetable material, which is attractive to bees, butterflies, moths and so on, which are in turn preyed on by birds. The following are good 'bird' plants for the herbaceous border: snapdragon, cornflower, forget-me-not, michaelmas daisy, evening primrose, pansy, cosmos, China aster, scabious, common field-poppy. The American chokeberry *Aronia melanocarpa*, produces brilliant autumn foliage along with huge black berries, which are eagerly taken by birds.

Roses

The rose family provides pretty, scented blooms that are largely unattractive to foraging birds, though if there are good numbers of hips these may be shredded by greenfinches looking for the seeds. The guelder rose *Viburnum opulus* produces clusters of red berries, which may be reluctantly taken by birds. It grows to 5.5m (18ft), but there is a cultivated version, *V. compactum,* which grows to 1.8m (6ft). The Japanese snowball *V. plicatum tomentosum* is sterile and useless from a bird's point of view. The wild rose *Rosa rugosa* produces good fruits, the seeds are much loved by greenfinches, and is much to be preferred to the more modern and showy varieties, which are selected for colour, shape and scent at the expense of anything which might please either bee or bird. In other words, cultivated roses are an abomination to the bird gardener. Let's hear it for the natives!

Lawns and lawn-watching

An open and well-kept lawn is a priceless asset to the bird-rich garden. It provides a courting arena for pigeons, a battleground for blackbirds, not to mention a great deal of choice food. Artificial and man-made though it may be, the green sward of the lawn, clearly observable and yet a constant attraction to bug, beast and bird, is a boon to the naturalist-gardener. Curious that this green invitation to laze and relax is the result of such brutal treatment to an inoffensive plant. The constant cutting down of its efforts to reach maturity is hard on the grass, and to add insult to injury, we cart off the cuttings to rot elsewhere, depriving the lawn of the very nutrients which aid its survival. Of course, these are replenished to a certain extent by the activity of soil bacteria and by the considerable efforts of worms, but over the years mowing will impoverish the soil if you deny it the cuttings. That is why, if you want to avoid bare patches, you need to import manures to counteract nitrogen deficiency. Again, if you cut too often and too close you will be providing conditions favourable to ground-hugging plants like dandelions, daisies and plantains. So give the grass a chance and keep the weeds in the shade, which doesn't suit them at all. Incidentally, the compost heap provides good pickings in that it is a hothouse of invertebrate-food production and a highly productive wormery. In winter its warmth may keep a small area free of snow and provide a welcome hunting ground.

Lawn-watching offers the easiest way of observing some of the different techniques used by birds for feeding. One of the constant wonders of the natural world is its diversity, the extraordinary range of plants and animals in any given habitat, and the way that they all manage to make a living by occupying slightly different niches.

A spectacular but rare spring visitor from the continent, searching lawns for insect larvae, the hoopoe may sometimes stay to breed.

Ornamental hoopoes

Gilbert White's delight in the birds and the wildlife of his home village of Selborne is well known. From the mundane to the unusual, the 18th-century curate recorded everything, but a highlight for him would also be a highlight for us more than 200 years later: 'The most unusual birds I ever observed in these parts were a pair of hoopoes (*upupa*) which came several years ago in the summer, and frequented an ornamented piece of ground, which joins to my garden'. Years ago hoopoes bred in a birdcage in Hampshire – I went to film them but they had flown …

Different lifestyles

Superficially, the 'nature red in tooth and claw' approach may seem justified, but it would be more accurate to see communities of different creatures living in tolerable harmony. Birds come in all shapes and sizes. Some hunt by day, some by night, some are vegetarian, some are meat eaters; some eat anything they can get hold of, including other birds. They may walk after their food, hop for it, fly for it, dive or swim for it. And each is specially equipped for the chosen job. One way or another anything that grows or moves gets eaten. Fruits, nuts, seeds, leaves, bark, living or decaying matter – all is grist to the mill. Very roughly, we can divide birds into four categories according to their beak shape: the hard-billed birds like sparrows, or finches, which have nutcracker bills; the soft-billed birds, like robins, which deal with insects; the dual-purpose bills, which take on all-comers; and the hook-billed predators like sparrowhawks.

Green woodpeckers – this one is a juvenile – search lawns for ants and ant nests.

On the lawn, the most obvious visitors are the birds searching for worms and soft grubs. The old saying about the early bird getting the worm is an exact observation of fact. Worms are creatures of moisture and mildness, early morning dew suits them, sunrise and sun warmth causes them to return underground. So thrushes and blackbirds comb the lawn at first light, and this is when you may see the biggest blackbird steal worms from the song thrush, thus getting his breakfast the easy way. Birds have a good sense of hearing, but they hunt almost entirely by the sense of sight, and to some extent touch – at least that is true of those most active by day. The frequent false observation that birds 'listen' for worms is based on a characteristic human weakness: people make the classic mistake of regarding birds, or any other animal for that matter, as if they, too, were people. The worm-hunting thrush hops a few paces, then stands very still and cocks its head to one side. A pause, and then the stab. So we deduce that the bird has its head cocked to listen for the sound of the worm. But the observer failed to note the fact that the bird's eye happens to be in the position where the human ear is found. When a man cocks his head in that attitude, he is listening intently. When a thrush does it, it is watching intently.

Blackbirds are bigger than thrushes, they may wait for the thrush to catch a worm and get their breakfast the easy way.

Watch the mole

There is another procedure that can produce good returns for birds. If a mole is busy at its underground activities, disturbing surface lines as it tunnels, thrushes and blackbirds will keep station on the mole, enjoying the worms that are displaced. This sort of activity, where one species benefits from the activities of another is known as commensalism.

The bird that is a universal favourite when it swoops on to a lawn is the green woodpecker, with its striking green plumage and red head. So remarkable is its appearance that many people find it difficult to believe that it is a British bird at all, working on the dismal assumption that home-grown species are bound to be dull and dowdy. But British it is, and a delight to see, working over the lawn and exploring for ants and ants' nests.

The other woodpeckers, equally striking in their red-and-white livery, are less likely to descend to ground level, but the green woodpecker, with its long, mobile tongue tipped with sticky mucus, searches out larvae from their hidey-holes in crevices. It may spear out larger bugs, but ants are its speciality.

Finch specialisms

Some of the lawn visitors are looking for grass and weed seeds, and of these perhaps the most attractive is the goldfinch. The sight of a charm of goldfinches attacking the golden dandelion ought to be enough to convert any gardener into a dandelion fan. They approach them with zest, leapfrogging on to stems, landing about halfway up towards the head so that they weigh it down to the ground. Then they get to work. All finches are seed-eaters, with powerful jaw muscles and bills modified for husking. Inside the bill they have two grooves, which lodge the nut or seed, then the tongue rotates it as the mandibles crush. The husk peels off, leaving the kernel to be swallowed. Different finches go for different seeds. A hawfinch, for example, is tough enough to cope with cherry and plum stones, which take some cracking. Goldfinches use their relatively long, narrow bills rather as a pair of tweezers, probing deep into the seedhead.

Although most of the time they are concerned with airborne flies, swallows will occasionally settle on a lawn to pick up flies if they are abundant. Lawns are the last part of the garden's structural jigsaw. The next chapter takes a closer look at the feeding stations and food we can put out to encourage the widest variety of birds.

Bird Tables

The most satisfying way of increasing the bird population in your garden is by growing the right kind of plants and creating as near a wild environment for birds as possible. But there is a great deal of pleasure to be derived from providing food in the most direct manner, by setting a dining table and serving suitable dishes. And almost any food you offer, from kitchen scraps to caviar, will be eaten by a wide variety of birds. By providing food you can entice the birds to show themselves more freely in places where you can watch them. And, as the availability of food controls (to a large extent) the bird population of your garden, you will also be increasing their numbers. But providing food is not a pleasure to undertake lightly. Put out some scraps and new residents will become dependent on your generosity, and if it fails they will be competing for an inadequate supply of natural foods. Especially in cold weather, birds may lose a lot of weight overnight, and they have to make it up again during the few hours of daylight. Death comes in a matter of hours even to a healthy small bird, if it is without food. In hard weather the real killer is hunger, not cold.

Early enthusiasts

While it is entirely possible to make out a case for feeding birds in order to improve their chances of survival, the reason most of us do it is because we enjoy involving ourselves in other creatures' lives and establishing closer relationships with them. St Francis of Assisi, born towards the end of the 12th century, was probably the first man to be credited with feeding birds from a relatively pure sense of goodwill. After a wild youth, he repented to take a vow of poverty and to devote his life to a form of pilgrimage, helping the poor. The poor, in this context, included the brute creation, which doubtless enjoyed the Franciscan's bounty without adopting his principles of poverty, chastity and obedience.

The first bird table

To the best of my knowledge, the first man to set up a bird table unselfishly dedicated to the sustenance of birds was John Freeman Dovaston, an early pioneer of field ornithology. In a letter to the artist Thomas Bewick in 1825, he mentioned his 'ornithotrophe', a feeding device which he had erected outside a window, to which he had enticed 23 species to take food on a snowy day. Over a quarter of a century later, the Rev. F. O. Morris, author of the highly successful and enjoyable, though somewhat patchy, *History of British Birds*, 1857, wrote letters to *The Times* encouraging people to put food out for the birds. But his request fell on fairly stony ground, since the thrifty Victorians didn't believe in admitting to waste of any kind, especially in the kitchen.

Peanut cages are very successful and preferable to net bags. They not only offer food, but they are also a venue for dramatic behaviour!

Birding feeding pioneers

In Germany, at about the same time, a wealthy landowner – the Baron von Berlepsch – was pioneering techniques of large-scale bird management. His primary interest was in the control of forest pests, but the aesthetics of bird encouragement played a significant part in his thinking. Despite the fact that his main efforts went into the development of nestboxes for woodland species (as we shall see in the next chapter) and that he underestimated the importance of food supply in relation to bird populations, he nevertheless experimented with the provision of artificial winter food supplies. His precise and demanding instructions for the erection and provision of 'food-houses' and 'food-bells' make fascinating reading. And he did much to encourage the spread of practical and unsentimental attitudes to the woolly world of bird preservation. His principal belief was that protection required an intimate knowledge of the birds' biology, and he held that Man's excesses had to be balanced by providing natural or near-natural conditions – thus von Berlepsch made it his business to lay down most precise requirements for his experiments. While he may have been somewhat over-demanding, his thinking was decidedly in advance of his times: 'a thorough and rational protection of birds is only possible where the representatives of agriculture and forestry join forces with those who are interested in birds from aesthetic and ethical motives, and work together for a common good. Unfortunately much energy is wasted in angry quarrels'. That could easily have been written today!

It was the long hard winter of 1890, which softened the British heart and induced large-scale bird feeding, especially in cities. By 1910, according to *Punch*, bird feeding had become a national pastime and commercial interests had begun to offer special furniture. Possibly the first person to suffer financially from the practice was brought to court during the latter stages of World War I, in the winter of 1916–17. Sophia Stuart was charged with wasting food, when a police sergeant found a quantity of bread cut into small pieces and scattered over the ground at the front and back of her house in Woking. He solemnly collected half a pound as evidence and charged the unfortunate woman. Mrs Stuart, an elderly woman who had lost her only son, claimed: 'the birds are my children, I have nothing else to love', and she stoutly informed the constable that she had fed the birds for years and proposed to continue. She insisted that she only used unclean crusts, and that it was not wasted if given to one's fellow creatures whether they went on two legs or four. In spite of her efforts, Mrs Stuart was found guilty and fined £2.

It would make an interesting exercise to work up a defence brief for Mrs Stuart, since she could have claimed that in feeding birds with scrap food she was working for the war effort. At any time, birds fulfil a vital role in the healthy functioning of our planet's system: as insect controllers, as agents of seed dispersal, as living barometers of ecological balance and, last but not least, as a primary food source. She should have claimed that she was ensuring the survival of useful allies!

The importance of feeding birds

Much has been made of the importance of feeding birds, especially in winter as a means of saving them from extinction, but most of the evidence won't stand serious consideration. Bird numbers are primarily controlled by the availability of their natural foods; artificial feeding can have only a marginal influence. Quite apart from the fact that it does have some practical effect, one reason for bird feeding is to use up kitchen scraps in a constructive manner. However, principally, the exercise gives us a lot of pleasure by attracting birds to a place where we see them to advantage. In really hard weather, extra feeding almost certainly saves a lot of individuals from an early grave. Famous ornithologist the late James Fisher once estimated that a million birds survived an exceptionally severe winter by courtesy of bird tables. Certainly feeding sustains a higher bird population in winter, at a time when the garden is at its least colourful, and that is a prime objective. Remember, though, that this sort of feeding is at best a substitute for natural food.

Hidden treasure

Standing wood decays in a different way from branches that have broken off and lie on the ground, which rot from the outside. Either way decaying wood provides essential food and habitat for fungi and invertebrates, birds feed on the bugs and can excavate nest holes into rotting trunks and branches. So treasure your dead wood – stumperies are all the gardening rage.

Interfering or helping?

Sometimes people claim that feeding birds is wrong because it interferes with the natural course of events. But the fact is that we interfere in the lives of our fellow creatures and vegetation in almost everything we do, and much of this activity is entirely proper. In any case the provision of a measure of food and water, together with a few nestboxes, represent a modest return for the loss of natural habitat we have inflicted on our wild neighbours. Taken to its logical conclusion, the 'antis' should go round knocking down the swallow and house martin nests built under our roofs in order to persuade these erring creatures to find themselves a more natural cliff or cave.

When there's snow on the bird table you can be sure the birds will appreciate your offerings. And don't forget to keep the bird bath ice-free!

In cold weather birds face several problems: the ground may be so hard that they cannot get at the invertebrate creatures of the soil; worms migrate downwards in dry or cold conditions; days are short, so hunting time is limited. Where there are streetlights, though, some birds such as blue tits, take advantage of the extra artificial light to work overtime and they forage almost without stopping in mid-winter. Provided birds' plumage is in good condition they are perfectly able to withstand low temperatures, but inevitably their energy requirement is increased as temperatures drop and they use fuel to keep them warm. Many birds lose ten per cent or more of their body weight overnight in cold weather, and the short daylight hours must produce food to replace the lost fat. While a large bird like a gull may manage comfortably for a couple of days, provided it can fill its belly with a decent fish from the fish quay or with some high-energy waste from a rubbish tip, a wren has an appetite that needs constant attention. Physically small, wrens have a proportionately large body surface and lose heat fast. Birds must maintain the highest body temperature of any animal – between 40°C and 44.4°C (104–112°F), as against Man's 37°C (98.6°F). And chemical reactions occur more rapidly at high temperatures. One way or another songbirds must work hard and fast at feeding.

Bird tables and their siting

The traditional way of feeding is with a bird table and, although it has limitations, it is on the whole a very satisfactory method. The table can either be supported on a post or it can hang from the bough of a tree, or a bracket. Your own situation will probably decide the method you use. There is little to choose between the two systems so long as you keep the cat problem firmly in mind and do not fix the hanging model to a potential cat-way.

Birds not only have varying food requirements, both in nature and at the bird table, but they also have varying methods of hunting. Some skulk about on the ground, some snoop along branches and foliage, and some run about on tree trunks and stone walls. So we must have variety of presentation as well as variety of food.

Some birds, such as blackbirds, thrushes, dunnocks and moorhens prefer to feed at ground level, so they are best fed from a suitable tray which is taken in at night to cheat the rats. Put the tray the best part of 2m (7ft) from the sort of cover that might hide a stalking cat. The greatest variety of bird species, however, come to visit a bird tray which is fixed 1.5m (5ft) or so off the ground, in a position where most of them will merely regard it as an unusually shaped tree branch. Tits, finches and robins will be the regular visitors, making a dozen or so everyday customers. There is great potential, too, for surprises when using this kind of tray, as we shall see later, and a fair chance of colourful visitors arriving – like woodpeckers, nuthatches and exotic creatures from Scandinavia and the Mediterranean. Even if your only contact with the outside world is by way of a window above ground-floor level, you have a fighting chance of seducing birds to take advantage of your offerings, depending of course on the kind of greenery there is in the neighbourhood.

Bird tables may be sited on a post or hanging from a branch (the birds won't mind the swaying!), but don't forget some birds prefer to feed at ground level.

The tray should offer a food surface of 40 × 20cm (16 × 8in). Naturally, there should be no easy access for cats. Therefore, ideally, the post should be made from a piece of water pipe which will probably prove too slippery for them to climb; or sheathed in a plastic tube, which has the same effect. A rustic pole merely invites cats and other predators to shin up and take pot luck! The worst monstrosity is the combination bird table and nestbox where any unfortunate owners of the nestbox are faced with an endless procession of callers, threatening their peace and causing territorial ructions.

Protection from weather and predators

If possible, the table should be protected from hot sun and driving winds; a roof is not essential, but has the advantage that it may keep off the worst of the rain. Some ornamental bird tables have the luxury of a thatched roof, which at least offers sparrows some useful nest material. If you have one of these, be careful it doesn't make access easier for squirrels and cats, which may jump from a nearby vantage point and find the thatch offers a good landing grip. In truth, it is almost impossible to defeat squirrels; they can solve the most fiendish problems of access to food.

The table should be sited carefully to afford good all-round vision to its visitors, while being 1.8m (6ft) or so from convenient cover. Birds will make use of convenient staging posts on their way to and from the bird table, so ensure these are available. If there are no suitable branches, provide some substitutes in the form of posts or horizontal perches.

It is important that the coaming framing the bird table has a few convenient gaps to allow odds and ends of crumbs to be swept away. Making a tray

Peanuts are a bird's best friend, but a variety of offerings is best of all.

is easy enough, but there is little doubt that the most practical bird table, offering good value for money, is the one sold by the RSPB (for address see page 178). Designed first and foremost from the point of view of the birds, it works well, and this is, after all, exactly what the human customer is looking for.

If you make your own table, check carefully that there are no sharp edges or protruding nails that might cut or damage the birds. Enclosing the feeding area with chicken wire will certainly keep starlings out, something which many people regard as desirable (not me!), but it has the undesirable effect of depriving access to thrushes, doves, and woodpeckers too. Probably the best solution is to provide food in a variety of ways, each allowing different birds a chance to get a share of the offerings. Scrap-cages, peanut baskets, seed globes and so on all have their uses, and in no time at all you will start to devise ingenious contraptions for defeating unwanted visitors. Or you could take the easy way and check the offerings from bird furniture suppliers (see page 180).

Other types of bird feeder

Nuthatches enjoy life upside down.

Bird-bells

It was the naturalist H. Mortimer Batten who made the half-coconut tit-bell famous, in the early days of radio on Children's Hour, and for many years a wooden version was made available to garden bird enthusiasts. In essence it is a very simple device, making it possible to use up kitchen scraps in a way that allows only the most agile birds to get them, with a certain amount of difficulty. Thus the 'greedy' starlings and sparrows were held at arm's length. The bell is turned upside down and placed in a mug or bowl and thus held firmly. It is primed with scraps and seeds, has a perch twig set in it, and is then filled with hot fat, though not the sort which stays liquid at room temperature (for recipe see page 46).

When the mixture has set, you hang the bell up for tits, nuthatches and woodpeckers to explore. One of the advantages of the bird-bell is that it lasts a long time between replenishments, so it keeps your birds happy if you have to go away. Even the ground-feeders get some benefit, when small pieces get dislodged and fall down. If you do not wish to buy one of the new terracotta versions you can make a perfectly good substitute from a half-coconut, the original and cheapest version!

Another useful hanging device is the suet stick. For this, bore 2.5cm (1in) holes through a short length of birch log, stuff the holes with raw beef or kidney suet and hang it up. Woodpeckers are very fond of this gadget; avoid fancy perches if you want to discourage other customers.

Suet is the way to a great spotted woodpecker's heart.

The guiding principle for successful bird table operation is to offer food in an enterprising variety of ways. If the feeding station ends up looking like a Christmas tree so much the better. Quite apart from the main dish offered on the table itself, there should be hanging baskets, seed hoppers, tit-bells and anything else you may think of. The object is to give as wide a range of foodstuffs in as wide a range of dishes as possible. Avoid collapsible or bouncy spiral wire feeders though, as they may trap a bird's leg while rebounding from the shock of its arrival.

Scrap baskets

Scrap baskets, in the form of a wire cage, are useful because they can be filled indoors at your convenience and the food doesn't get scattered about quite so freely as with the bird table. But, like the peanut bags, they cannot be used by all birds. So, it is important to spread your largesse by way of a variety of feeding stations and devices.

Suet is another high-energy food. It is ideal for presenting in scrap baskets or it melts down well for tit-bell use. The short variety is more appropriate than the stringy and it serves as an acceptable substitute for the fat grubs and insects which woodpeckers enjoy. Stuffed into mesh bags, or scrap baskets, or stuck into crevices and crannies on tree trunks, it will act as a magnet for colourful birds like great spotted woodpeckers and welcome visitors like long-tailed tits. The brilliantly coloured woodpeckers are relatively recent bird table addicts, having first taken to the practice some time in the late 1950s.

Grit for the gizzard

It may be worth putting out a small quantity of grit – fine sand, gravel or even small bits of coal – to aid the avian digestion process. It makes sense to provide a small amount on, or under, the bird table.

Now they are common visitors to feeding stations. Incidentally, like treecreepers, they are fond of uncooked pastry. If you cram suet into the crevices of an old, gnarled Scots pine, it will attract other visitors as well as woodpeckers and treecreepers – for instance, goldcrests and even firecrests, together with wintering chiffchaffs and blackcaps.

Varieties of food

Different birds have different food requirements and different search patterns for satisfying them. This is, after all, the main reason that they manage to coexist so successfully. Therefore, the shrewd bird gardener studies his potential bird list, and supplies and serves food accordingly. Some species are primarily vegetarian, some are seed-eaters, some are carnivorous and some like a bit of everything. If you take a look at a bird's foraging tools you will straight away have a fair idea of what it needs. Finches have nutcracker bills, adapted to crack and crush, and they feed mostly on grain and seeds. They are hard-billed. Robins and wrens have slender bills designed for the delicate process of probing for grubs, caterpillars and other insects. They are called soft-billed birds. Hawks have hooked bills for tearing flesh. Gulls have general-purpose bills.

Birds eat an astonishing variety of items, though by and large they do have a decided order of preference. Thrushes prefer the rich meat of worms, but will take snails or fruit as second best. Blackbirds search for worms in the first light of dawn, only later resorting to the bird table. Natural food is clearly the best for them, and if possible this is what should be provided on the bird table and the ground feeding tray. Rowan berries, elderberries, crab apples, hazel and almond nuts, boiled conkers, sweet chestnuts,

BIRDS THAT VISIT FEEDING STATIONS

An amazing range of birds has been recorded at feeding stations. You might be more than a little surprised to find a dipper or a kingfisher in most gardens, but the prospect of the unexpected is one of the thrills of birdwatching, as you can see by the birds in this list of birds recorded in gardens.

Blackbird	Goldcrest	Partridge, Red-legged	Thrush, Mistle
Blackcap	Goldfinch	Pheasant	Thrush, Song
Brambling	Goose, Canada	Pigeon, Feral	Tit, Bearded
Budgerigar	Goose, Pink-footed	Pigeon, Wood	Tit, Blue
Bullfinch	Goshawk	Pipit, Meadow	Tit, Coal
Bunting, Cirl	Greenfinch	Rail, Water	Tit, Great
Bunting, Corn	Gull, Black-headed,	Redpoll, Lesser	Tit, Marsh
Bunting, Reed	Gull, Herring	Redwing	Tit, Long-tailed
Bunting, Snow	Hawfinch	Ring-necked Parakeet	Tit, Willow
Canary	Heron, Grey	Robin	Treecreeper
Chaffinch	Jackdaw	Rook	Turnstone
Chiffchaff	Jay	Shelduck	Wagtail, Pied
Crossbill	Kestrel	Siskin	Wheatear
Crow, Carrion	Kingfisher	Sparrow, House	Woodpecker, Great spotted
Dipper	Linnet	Sparrow, Tree	Woodpecker, Green
Dove, Collared	Magpie	Sparrowhawk	Woodpecker, Lesser spotted
Dove, Rock	Mallard	Starling	Wren
Dunnock	Merlin	Swan, Mute	Yellowhammer
Fieldfare	Moorhen		
Firecrest	Partridge, Grey		

acorns and beechmast are all highly suitable, though it will be more convenient for your guests if you crush, or chop and grate the harder nuts.

Thrushes will gladly take your fruit straight from the tree, but may well be diverted if you are able to offer rejected fruit collected from your local fruiterer. Squash it first; it will be much appreciated in cold weather. If you can go to the expense of buying commercially prepared food, then the various mixes will be a great success. And peanuts please almost every kind of bird. Kitchen scraps are not only taken by the obvious 'general purpose' birds like starlings but also by the specialist insect-eaters like blackcaps, chiffchaffs, treecreepers, and woodpeckers. Seed-eating birds like linnets, corn buntings, lesser redpolls, to say nothing of tawny owls and herons, are also attracted. All these, and many others, have patronized well-stocked bird tables. (For addresses of bird food suppliers see page 180.)

Try experimenting and remember that any left-over delicacies such as stilton rind, Christmas pudding or even haggis will be gratefully received. The only things to avoid are salted, highly spiced, dehydrated foods. Make the offerings of either a size large enough to discourage birds from carrying them away to drop for the rats to find, or small enough to be eaten on the spot.

In a hard winter we may welcome Scandinavian thrushes, redwings and fieldfares, to windfall fruit.

A mixed bunch of customers – chaffinch, brambling and a couple of bullfinches.

Good bread

Bread is a controversial subject. Many people argue heatedly (and wrongly) that it should not be offered on bird tables. There are certainly dangers to avoid. Dry bread may swell inside the bird's crop and choke it, so be careful to make it moist (sparrows, and others, are careful to dunk dry bread before eating it). One solution is to soak the crumbs in bacon grease, which will be appreciated. (And here is the good news about white bread: the incidence of beri-beri in London's street pigeons was all but eliminated when they began enjoying the modern vitamin-enriched sliced bread. Make of that what you will.) One garden-bird enthusiast compiled a list of the birds he had seen taking bread in the outer suburbs of London, and they totalled 23 – including mallard; herring, common, black-headed and lesser black-backed gulls; feral and woodpigeons; carrion crow; jay; great, blue and coal tits; song thrush; blackbird; robin; dunnock; starling; skylark; greenfinch; chaffinch; siskin; house and tree sparrows. Doubtless more will join the list. At a popular bird-feeding place by a car park in a woodland area of Humberside, long-tailed tits joined the queue for white bread crumbs. I once enticed a wild whooper swan to come to 'Mother's Pride' over a period of weeks. So there may be a few surprises, and a lot of delights, in store for us all.

Feeding finches

Finches present something of a problem in that they prefer seeds, and seeds are expensive and extraordinarily difficult to serve without scattering. If they are offered in a mixed variety then the birds will throw them all over the place as they search diligently for those they like best. Seeds also need to be kept dry, of course. Seed hoppers are notoriously ineffective, but the 'Droll Yankee' or 'Defender' range of tube-feeders work well. They are designed to dispense seed mixtures of the 'special mix' type from a generous reservoir. One model offers greenfinches tiers of perches so that a whole flock of birds can feed simultaneously.

Many of the seeds from a seed hopper find their way to the ground below. Not all are eaten by ground-feeders. Some may lie there and, in time, germinate and sprout into an exotic garden of unexpected plants. One distinguished botanist carried out some fascinating experiments in which, instead of offering commercial bird food to the birds, he planted it. He was puzzled by the strange names which were given by the seedsmen, and found after much research, that seeds called 'blue maw' and 'dari', which are not found in botanical books, revealed themselves to be the opium poppy *Papaver*

Odd colours

Strangely coloured birds in your garden may well be a variation of a common species rather than an exotic visitor. For example, red seed-eating birds that made regular visits to a bird feeder in a Scottish garden turned out to be house sparrows whose unusual colour was attributed to their feeding on a store of fish food that contained prawn shells. In spring, blackbirds on Tresco in the Isles of Scilly have brilliant scarlet heads after feeding on exotic plants.

somniferum and the annual tropical cereal *Sorghum bicolor* when they were encouraged to grow into plants. Often enough the ground under a bird feeding station will blossom with brilliant sunflowers.

Peanuts

Peanuts are almost the perfect produce for the dedicated feeder – whether human, bird or device! Convenient to handle, store and serve, they are energy-packed with a high calorie content. But buy 'safe nuts', carrying the recommendation of the BirdCare Standards Association, not mouldy ones that have turned yellow, as they may be highly poisonous, producing aflatoxin, a toxin that kills the liver cells and has caused the death of many garden birds. Unshelled peanuts will be eaten by a variety of species. Offered freely, they will be used up at the rate of several pounds a week, therefore it is best to present them in cages that encourage the birds to work at the job of freeing them.

Strung, in their shells, they provide amusement for us as we watch the acrobatic tits breaking and entering. But be careful that you don't string them on multi-thread cotton which might tangle up their feet. Tits may perch on the bird table to haul up a string of nuts 'bill over claw', a version of the natural behaviour whereby they pull twigs closer to them inspect them for caterpillars.

Escaped cage birds that have established themselves in the wild in the south-east, ring-necked parakeets hail from south Asia. Fruit and nut eaters, they are happy to patronize bird tables.

BIRD SEEDS REVEALED

Seedmen's names, translated and revealed in the periodical *New Scientist*.

Aniseed *Pimpinella anisum*	Japanese millet *Echinochloa utilis*
Blue maw *Papaver somniferum*	Plate yellow millet *Panicum miliaceum*
Buckwheat *Fagopyrum esculentum*	White millet *P. miliaceum*
Mazagan canary *Phalaris canariensis*	Niger *Guizotia abyssinica*
Chicory *Cichorium intybus*	Panicum millet *Setaria italica*
Dari *Sorghum bicolor*	Black rape *Brassica campestris*
Gold of pleasure *Camelina sativa*	German rubsen *B. campestris*
Hemp *Cannabis sativa*	Chinese safflower *Carthamnus tinctorius*
White kardi *Carthamnus tinctorius*	Black sunflower seed *Helianthus annuus*
White lettuce *Lactuca sativa*	Striped sunflower seed *Helianthus annuus*
Best Dutch linseed *Linum usitassimum*	French teasel *Dipsacus sylvestris*
Chinese millet *Setaria italica*	

The spread of siskins

Tits and greenfinches are the prime customers for peanuts, but other species take advantage of the titbits that fall to the ground. Dunnocks, and on occasion bramblings, will forage below while as many as three species of tit and greenfinches are working above. Robins are fond of peanuts, too, and although they find some difficulty in fluttering alongside and grabbing a morsel, they can manage it. Jays, chaffinches and, indeed, bramblings, have all learnt to enjoy the bounty of the peanut cage. One of the most remarkable instances of a bird expanding its range through a liking for peanuts is that of the siskin, a small acrobatic finch once associated with Forestry Commission conifer plantations, where they enjoy spruce and pine seeds in spring and summer.

> **WARNING**
>
> Avoid any peanut feeder that involves a flexible coiled-spring system. These are highly dangerous, since one bird may get its feet jammed when another bird flies away from the feeder causing the spring to contract. Also avoid all-in-one nest-box/feeding-tray/water/trough devices. It is asking for trouble to invite birds to eat or drink at the doorstep to another bird's house, creating territorial stresses and strains.

Originally confined to the Caledonian pine forest of Scotland, they slowly extended south from the mid-19th century, colonizing parkland and conifer forests and reaching North Wales, Norfolk and the New Forest a hundred years later. Then, some thirty years ago, they started to come into gardens and feed on peanuts in south-east England. The habit has now spread through most of the country and the numbers wintering have increased, till nowadays we see them feeding on tideline seed debris on the Exe Estuary in Devon, for example.

Siskins display a curious preference for peanuts offered in the small red plastic netting containers like those used by greengrocers for packing carrots, coming readily to gardens with these bags rather than the conventional scrap-cages, demonstrating bad judgment on their part. And furthermore, it has been confidently asserted that they prefer these red mesh bags to any other device. These birds are not only from the increasing British breeding population, but also from Scandinavia and the Baltic. Their

Siskins first became attracted to gardens in spring by peanuts in the much disapproved of red netbags. Normal diet is conifer seeds.

numbers fluctuate widely from year to year, but are generally at their highest in March and early April just before they migrate back to their breeding grounds – either in northern Britain or across the North Sea.

Long-tailed tits at a scrap bag.

Those winters when few siskins are seen probably coincide with good seed crops nearer to their breeding grounds.

Coconut shells

Tits are the family that gives the greatest pleasure to house-bound birdwatchers who simply enjoy the company of their birds. Their acrobatics are always a joy to watch, and they display a touching enthusiasm for any feeding device that offers nuts or fat. Blue tits have a tendency to examine everything in the hope that it might be edible. They will strip putty from window frames, they will tear wallpaper to see what's behind it – all versions of their natural behaviour in turning leaves over in the hope of finding a bug on the underside. They very much enjoy coconut, which should be put out fresh, in the shell. Just saw the nut in half and suspend it so the rain doesn't spoil the flesh.

SUITABLE BIRD TABLE FOOD

Animal fats *good for warblers, tits, robins, woodpeckers and nuthatches*

Suet *beef best, or mutton*

Marrow bones *cracked, but not cooked bones, which might be eaten by dogs or foxes, when the splinters may stick in their stomachs*

Bacon rinds *short pieces*

Chicken carcass *try hanging it from a tree*

Tinned pet food

Mealworms

Maggots

Ants' eggs

Cheese *grated, small*

Hard-boiled egg

Fruit *for thrushes, etc. fresh, dried or decaying*

Berries *of all sorts*

Nuts *of all sorts*

Peanuts *not salted*

Almonds

Hazel

Brazils *for nuthatches, jam them in a tree crevice*

Seeds

Mixed *i.e. special mix, see page 180 for suppliers*

Hemp *a 'best buy' but must be kept dry – taken by greenfinches, bullfinches and buntings, nuthatches, woodpeckers*

Canary seed *for chaffinches*

Millet

Maize

Niger

Corn

Melon

Sunflower seed *heaven for greenfinches*

Rice

Potato *boiled or baked in jacket*

Stale cake crumbs

Coconut *in shell, not desiccated*

Uncooked pastry *treecreepers like it*

Biscuit crumbs

Breadcrumbs

Oats *coarse, but raw, not offered as porridge, which is glutinous and sticks to plumage and bills*

Feeding times

It is probably best to feed at regular times, morning and late afternoon for instance, or better still, first thing in the morning only. If you have to go away be sure to leave freshly filled tit-bells and seed hoppers which keep the birds occupied until your return. Keep feeding right through the winter and remember that it is especially important to provide seeds for your finches in the spring, at a time when they are not very abundant naturally.

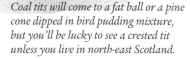

Coal tits will come to a fat ball or a pine cone dipped in bird pudding mixture, but you'll be lucky to see a crested tit unless you live in north-east Scotland.

There has been much controversy about the advisability of putting out bird table food during the breeding season. The best informed opinion seems to be that while adult birds are perfectly capable of deciding what is good for them, it is possibly best to provide peanuts in such a way that they cannot be carried whole to the nest. Crush them or offer only in mesh feeders. Summer feeding has become ever more important as farmland has become less attractive to wild birds. Gardens offer a vital piece in the feeding jigsaw.

Bullfinches have a catholic diet, they take seeds, berries, buds, shoots and bugs. In a hard winter, when their preferred food of ashmast has been scarce, they may ravage fruit tree buds in spring.

Birds appreciate help in the breeding season too, when young are clamouring for food, as much as in the hard days of winter when their main concern is to keep themselves alive. In the breeding season you can also offer nest material by stuffing peanut cages and scrap baskets with straw and feathers, dog or cat combings, short bits of cotton and bits of cotton wool.

A songbird will look markedly different before and after the nesting season. After bringing up one or two clutches of hungry juveniles, it may well appear the worse for wear, so the moult offers a welcome chance for a new suit of clothes. Food deficiencies may sometimes affect plumage, especially round the head where there may be a few bare patches. This will be a signal for you to increase the allowance of B-complex vitamins on the bird table: give a little bit of cheese!

Recipes from the Cordon Oiseau School of Cookery

Cakes and puddings for the bird table

Basic pud

Take seeds, peanuts, cheese, oatmeal, dry cake and scraps. Put them in a container, pour hot fat over the mixture until it is covered, and leave to set. Turn out on to a table, unless you have prepared it in a tit-bell or coconut holder. Rough quantities: 400g (1lb) of mixture to 200g (8oz) of melted fat.

Another basic pud

200g (8oz) beef suet   50–75g (2–3oz) flour
300g (12oz) coarse oatmeal   125g (5oz) water
Mix flour and oatmeal with liquid fat and water to stiff paste. Bake in shallow pie dish to form flat cake at 175°C (350°F) for approximately one hour.

Yet another pudding

Boil together one cup of sugar and one cup of water for five minutes. Mix with one cup of melted fat (suet, bacon or ordinary shortening), and leave it to cool. Then mix with breadcrumbs, flour, bird seed, a little boiled rice and scraps, until the mixture is very stiff. Pack into any kind of tin can or glass jar. Lay the can on its side in a tree, on the window sill, or any place where birds can perch and pick out the food. The can must be placed securely so that the birds cannot dislodge it, nor rain get inside.

Miss Turner's maize cake

Miss Turner was a pioneer bird gardener. In her book *Every garden a bird sanctuary* (Witherby 1935) she wrote 'feeding and watching birds is a sport'.
  Mix 100g (3oz) maize meal in a bowl with equal quantities of chopped nuts, hemp, canary and millet seed. Stir with boiling water till coagulated, and add two beaten eggs. Tie tightly in a cloth and bake at 175°C (350°F) for 50 minutes to one hour.

Bird cake

1kg (2lb) self-raising flour
200g (8oz) margarine
a little sugar
Mix with water and bake like a rock bun.

Fillings for bird-bells, suet sticks and pine cones

Basic tit-bell recipe

Fill the upturned bell with seeds, peanuts, cheese, oatmeal, sultanas, cake crumbs and other scraps. Pour in hot fat to the brim. Insert a short piece of twig into the mix to act as a learner's perch, if necessary. Leave to harden. Turn the bell over and hang in a suitable place where small birds like blue tits are already accustomed to come for food. The bell works best in cold weather.

Another tit-bell mix, equally suitable for open offer on the bird table, comprises seeds, peanuts, oatmeal, cake crumbs and cheese. Put them in a container (bird-bell, baking dish), pour hot fat to cover. Leave to set. In the case of an open tray, simply turn it out on to the bird table. Bacon or sausage fat is ideal, using 200g (8oz) of melted fat to 500g (1lb) of mix, very roughly.

Bill Oddie mix

Mix stale cake and fat with a few dried currants and sultanas.

Imprisoned in a 12.5–20cm (5–8in) wire-mesh bag, it keeps birds busy and prevents too much scatter.

The Baron Von Berlepsch food-tree recipe

This mix was formulated by the good Baron as a means of extending the plenteous times of summer to woodland birds in winter, and provides high-energy, intensive feeding. It was to be poured, hot, on to either the branches of a live young conifer or an imitation tree made of separate branches. Since living trees promptly lost their leaves – the needles – when hot fluids were poured on them, he recommended this practice only in the sort of woodlands that could suffer the sight of an ugly and diseased tree. In more sensitive areas, he suggested using a felled tree, imported for the purpose. While still enjoying the Baron's recipes a century later, I think we may take it for granted that the birds will not fuss too much over the method of presentation, and this recipe serves well as a bird-bell mix. The Baron tells us that it is by no means necessary to keep closely to the ingredients; it is only to serve as a guide, though a large part of the mix should always consist of hemp:

150g (5oz) breadcrumbs	75g (3oz) hemp seed, whole or crushed
75g (3oz) millet seeds	40g (1½oz) sunflower seeds
40g (1½oz) oats	50g (2oz) ants' eggs
40g (1½oz) dried elderberries	Suet (beef suet), the less stringy the better

Mix well, fill the bell and bind with hot, melted suet. Cool. Add more suet, melt and cool again. The second time of cooling produces a harder consistency. This mix offers high calorific value to birds that have difficulty in finding their preferred insect diet in winter.

Mealworm culture

(Robins will thank you for your efforts here.) Take a smooth-sided container such as a large circular biscuit tin or one of those out-dated and highly unsuitable glass bowls traditionally used for unfortunate goldfish. An open top provides plenty of air, but have a wire mesh lid which will foil escape attempts.

Put a 10–15cm (4–6in) layer of dry wheat bran or barley meal in the bottom, then a layer of hessian sacking. Add a vegetable layer of carrot, turnip, banana and apple skins, dry bread, raw potato, cabbage, as available – but ensure that the medium does not become too wet as it will then ferment, smell appalling and probably kill the mealworms. A good productive mixture will not smell.

Then take more hessian sacking and add more vegetable/bran layers to produce a multi-tier sandwich of mealworm delight. Introduce 200–300 mealworms (mealworms from an aviculturist's pet shop, not a fishing shop's maggots) and keep in a warm room.

After a few weeks the mealworms, fat and happy, will turn into creamy pupae, then into little black beetles, which represent your breeding stock. They lay eggs, which hatch into mealworms, and so on. Crop the mealworms in accordance with the scientific principles of MSY – maximum sustainable yield – in other words, make sure you keep a viable breeding stock. (If you want to start an empire, prepare other tins and prime them with a few bits of dry bread from an existing colony. These will carry beetle eggs.)

Some weeks later the mealworm city will be reduced to a dry powder, and you then need to renew the vegetable layers and bran. You may also find it useful to feed your worms with a slice of damp bread every week. Fold a sheet of paper into a concertina and place this on top of the mix; this will serve as a resting place for mealworms and simplify collection.

Serve the mealworms in a fairly deep, round dish, so that they cannot escape – they are surprisingly mobile. Gentles are sometimes recommended but, though I have not tasted them myself and the birds certainly like them, they are less wholesome to handle than mealworms. (Gentles are fly maggots, whereas mealworms are the larval form of the beetle *Tenebrio molitor*.)

Earthworm culture

Earthworms, *Lumbricus terrestris,* are bisexual, each individual exhibiting both male and female characteristics. But it still needs two to start a family. Use a suitable box in a shady position. Fill with a mixture of sand, well-ground manure (which may include a generous helping of household peelings and greens), rich loamy soil and peat moss in equal parts. Water and mix well. Turn and sprinkle with yet more water every few days. Introduce your breeding stock after two weeks, when the mix has cooled to between 19°C and 24°C (66–75°F). In three months you will have a powerhouse of worm production, to be culled for your ground-feeders' tray.

Or you can buy your worms or mealworms from Wiggly Wigglers! (see page 180).

Establishing a hierarchy

A well-supplied bird table will be a delight to watch, especially in winter when it is fulfilling its main purpose. A continuous stream of finches and tits will share the pickings with starlings, sparrows and perhaps even woodpeckers and nuthatches. There will be much interest in putting names to the birds, in sorting out their plumages (and later in the summer in watching the spotty juveniles adopt their adult flying suits). But there will also be interest in watching behaviour at the bird table. Some species will appear tolerant of all-comers, some will object strongly – even to the company of their own kind. Both robins and blackbirds, for instance, may hold their breeding territories through the winter, and do not encourage trespass. Blue tits and greenfinches, by contrast, enjoy a daily round where they may visit a whole series of different gardens. There is a suggestion that some great tits are developing a tendency to sit tight in garden territories, possibly encouraged by the availability of bird table food.

Pecking orders

Study the behaviour of your breakfast guests over a period of time, and you should be able to work out a pecking order. Birds are easily inclined to quarrel over their food, and these feeding squabbles are well observed at the bird table, where they inevitably come into close contact. One threatens another by posturing, i.e. gaping aggressively, spreading wings and tail. It is largely a game of bluff, since neither individual wants to come to blows, wasting energy and risking the loss of precious feathers, to say nothing of the danger from predators if they aren't keeping a proper watch. But the game has a serious object, because the winner gets the choicest titbit (and at other times, the best perch, the best breeding territory and the most desirable mate). So the establishment of a pecking order is a meaningful affair, and it plays a real part in everyday bird life, to say nothing of our own.

The peck order, or, more scientifically, dominance hierarchy, is so called because the experimental work which demonstrated its validity was

Blackbirds are noisy fighters, as they establish their place in the pecking order.

carried out with domestic hens. They establish dominance by pecking about the head and shoulders of rivals. It applies to species that live social or colonial lives, involving a great deal of shoulder-rubbing with other birds, not necessarily of their own species. The process, involving fights, bickering and bluff, continues until an order emerges. From the boss birds downwards, everyone knows his place, though bickering is constant, with individuals jostling and 'trying it on' with the object of improving their rating. The dominant cock has it all his own way, eating the best food and fathering the most chicks on the most attractive hens. He therefore leads an aggressive life, defending and consolidating his position till he is inevitably toppled as age creeps up on him. In a mixed flock there will still be a peck order, which explains why the 'greedy' starling takes precedence at the bird table, followed in the hierarchy by house sparrows, great, blue, marsh or willow and coal tits in that order. In fact blue tits will rob great tits almost as often as they are robbed by them, but these two species dominate the other tits, with coal tits the weakest in the hierarchy.

A starling takes precedence on this suet block; a blackcap and great tit feed further down ...

Starlings are aggressive and quarrelsome by nature; it is one of the traits which led them to earlier success, in population terms at least if not in terms of our approbation, till their recent decline. This can be seen as they work over a garden lawn, but is most obvious at the bird table, where the constraints of space, and the stimulus of abundant food, work them up to fever pitch. Working fast, they grab the biggest bits and, in their anxiety to get away from a potentially dangerous situation, they scatter food far and wide. In early spring, the sexes are easily distinguishable, the males having blue-grey at the base of the bill where females show pink. Armed with this knowledge you will soon see that the males are the ones feeding on plenty at the bird table, while the submissive females are banished to less attractive places.

... while the pied wagtail prefers to gather the crumbs that have fallen to the ground.

Winter feeders

Birds derive advantage from the autumn plenty by putting on fat and by laying up a winter store. It is in autumn, when berries and seeds are plentiful, that you are least likely to have a well-attended bird table – the natural food available is a greater attraction. But it may be that your bird table is not particularly successful in a winter which follows a bumper seeding season. In other words, there is no substitute for natural food, and birds will prefer it given a choice. As well as seeds, there will still be a measure of life-support in the hibernating flies, spiders, woodlice, centipedes and so on, which find just enough warmth to overwinter in the fallen leaves of undergrowth. One of the characteristic sounds of winter is the crunching noise made by foraging blackbirds as they thunder about in the shrubbery, foraging.

It is in a hard winter, when the extreme cold requires more energy output by birds to maintain their body temperatures, that the bird table is a life-saver. The most obvious effect of the arrival of a cold snap is that more species will come for the food. There will be mistle thrushes, greenfinches, long-tailed tits, and more blackbirds. Fieldfares and redwings will visit the garden and the bird table, and there will be bramblings feeding under the nut cages for fallen morsels. In extreme conditions, even the fiercely territorial robins will feed side by side. Other species will find their way in from exposed country to enjoy the relative shelter, including reed buntings and yellowhammers, grey wagtails, skylarks and meadow pipits, pheasants and moorhens. Wrens may take crumbs from bird tables in a way that is entirely untypical.

A great tit feeding on a bird pudding mix.

Welcome guests

It is perhaps true that the existence of bird table food has made it possible for some normally migrant birds to stay with us and endure our British winter. Blackcaps, which are overwintering in increasing numbers, mostly in the mild south and south-west, are particularly vulnerable to severe winters. They rely heavily on berries, such as those of *Cotoneaster* and honeysuckle, will eat the holly berries which are not exactly popular generally, and turn to ivy berries as their preferred food. Rotting windfall apples are also important to them, and they have even been seen to take mistletoe berries, a fruit which seems of little interest to most birds. It is in hard weather that blackcaps are most likely to be seen at bird tables, looking for cake crumbs, fat, nuts and seeds, and this is the time when a tray of rejected fruit from

the shop will be most welcome.
Overwintering chiffchaffs will come to
the bird table, too, for crumbs and suet.

It is possible that bird table offerings
fuelled the range expansion of that
exotic invader, the ring-necked parakeet.
This attractive looking parrot,
originating from Africa and India,
escaped from captivity, or was perhaps
deliberately released in some numbers
(as a human response to its unrewarding
behaviour in captivity), at the end of the
1960s. Since then, starting from a
nucleus in the London suburbs and Kent,
it has slowly but surely colonized the south-
east and established itself as a feral species and
something of a pest. Omnivorous by nature, it
prefers fruit and has a devastating effect on apple
orchards with its tendency to take just a couple of
pecks at each fruit. It comes freely to bird tables
and, breeding in tree holes, will presumably take to
nestboxes. Even the most severe winters have failed
to halt its spread, in spite of predictions that it
could not survive the cold. Broadly speaking, it is true
that birds are perfectly able to withstand the lowest
temperatures, provided they are well fed and protected
by healthy plumage.

*Bird table food and
garden berries encourage
blackcaps to overwinter
in Britain. This one is
enjoying white bryony.*

Water needs

In extreme winter conditions, when water is frozen and mudflats
glazed by ice, water birds and waders suffer greatly. Herons and
kingfishers must go down to the sea to find open water; pied
wagtails cannot find their ditchside insects; thrushes and robins
cannot penetrate the frozen earth. And small birds like long-tailed
tits, wrens and goldcrests may die because there aren't enough feeding
hours in the day for them to meet their high energy requirements.
So, once you start operating a winter bird table, it is of the utmost
importance that you keep it well supplied through the dark months
and, indeed, on into summer.

Sparrows and starlings in trouble

Among the results for the last couple of winters from the British Trust for Ornithology's Garden Bird Feeding Survey (see page 63) is that the house sparrow and the starling have taken a lower place than in the past. Numbers using gardens have dropped, evidence that both species are in serious decline.

House sparrows are omnivorous and are a successful species by virtue of the very fact that they have specialized in living as mess-mates with humans. They are tough customers at the bird table, scattering food about in a tiresome manner and ousting all non-sparrow competition.

Bright birds

Not many years ago sparrows were foiled by hanging mesh baskets of the sort designed for tits. The sparrows showed interest in them and fluttered alongside ineffectively, but failed to get a grip on the mesh. As the years went by they learnt to grasp the side of the basket and pick out the nuts in greenfinch fashion. Now this habit is widespread. House sparrows are versatile performers, taking seeds from seedheads in the manner of a goldfinch, working over trees like a woodpecker and hawking for flying insects like a flycatcher. Until recently they seemed invincible, but the last ten years have seen a serious decline in their numbers for reasons which are not yet fully understood. Farm regulations, which mean that grain stores are now sealed, have deprived them of one of their regular feeding places, but the general intensification of farming and, in towns, shortage of insect food at the critical time when chicks are in the nest, may be involved. Sparrows need all the help they can get.

Chequered career

Farm practices are also probably the cause of the decline in starlings, depriving parents of fat invertebrates at a time when the chicks are in need of them, inevitably leading to poor breeding success. Starlings have had a chequered career as British birds. Two hundred years ago they occurred only in the remotest parts of Scotland and Ireland, and only in the 20th century did they colonize the rest of Britain and south-east Ireland. Now they seem on the brink of change in distribution again.

House sparrows are pugnacious birds, bullying others, like blue tits, and taking command of any food source.

Birding from the kitchen window

A large window or conservatory can make a ready-made hide from which to watch your garden visitors in comfort, often providing astonishingly close-up views. Curtains or slatted vertical blinds will help to make a screen so that the smallest movement from within does not scare the birds away, and should also help to prevent birds from flying straight into them in sometimes fatal error.

Unusual garden visitors

One of the pleasures of bird table watching is the slow but steady way in which more and more species are being lured to feeding stations. Not only kestrels, sparrowhawks (and even red kites in some areas where they are becoming re-established), but more and more of the birds which formerly kept us at some distance have been recorded. Great spotted woodpeckers and long-tailed tits are more common visitors than they once were. Goldcrests, firecrests, cirl buntings, woodcock, common snipe, water rail, kingfishers and dippers – all are species that have taken to the habit of visiting feeding stations. Bearded tits have been encouraged to visit seed piles near reedbeds at the Minsmere RSPB reserve. Little gulls have taken food scraps from a litter bin. It seems there is no limit to the possibilities.

Birds of the night and difficult to see, woodcocks will spend the day in dense cover, yet they have been seen at garden feeding stations as ground feeders.

Goldcrests prefer conifers but are among many species that have taken to visiting feeding stations.

Where you live will, of course, have a considerable bearing on your potential bird list. Sailors at sea have operated bird feeding stations for many years. On migration, many land birds have sought respite on weather ships and oil rigs, as well as ships steaming at sea. Kestrels visited a weather ship at Station India, stayed three days and were fed on steak. A little auk was once desperate enough to take tinned sardines. Bramblings and snow buntings were seen at 71° South and 74° North respectively. A great blue heron landed on the flight deck of HMS *Hermes*, of Falklands fame, when she was 800km (500 miles) east of Puerto Rico in the Caribbean, and was entertained on the quarterdeck for two days with dishes of pilchards. The cargo vessel

Sugar Crystal was joined 225km (140 miles) south-west of Ireland, while on passage to Felixstowe, by 34 jackdaws and three rooks, which squabbled over grain spillage on the decks. On a more everyday level, no cross-Channel yachtsman can have failed to have the company, at some time or another, of a tired racing pigeon looking for a rest and some sustenance.

Clever crows and wise owls

Not surprisingly, given their widely regarded aptitude and intelligence, members of the crow family have learnt the advantages of artificial food. Magpies, as part of a general increase in numbers, have become more common in country gardens as well as the suburbs, where there is a scarcity of gamekeepers. First they took the songbirds' eggs and young, and then moved in to take the food provided for them. Though it may be something of a strain for the bird enthusiast to see magpies culling his hard-won neighbours, one just has to sit back and let them act as healthy predators and sort things out amongst themselves. So far the evidence is that they do not affect songbird populations adversely.

Jays will collect unshelled peanuts and carry them off for burying and subsequent digging up as a food store, in the same way that they bury vast numbers of acorns in the autumn.

Food storage is also typical of other species, such as nuthatches and the tits, which hide food at a time when it is abundant, but it is particularly widespread amongst the crow family. It occurs when there is more food about than the birds are able to eat, and quite apart from obviously suitable items like nuts, they will hide bread or cheese pieces. This family propensity to store food gave rise to the 'thieving magpie' legend. And while wild birds do not carry off gold rings and diamond necklaces, it is highly likely that tame ones might do so when they are deprived of their natural foraging. The tawny is the most common garden owl (barn owls prefer uninhabited buildings). Well adapted to suburban life, it has learnt to become

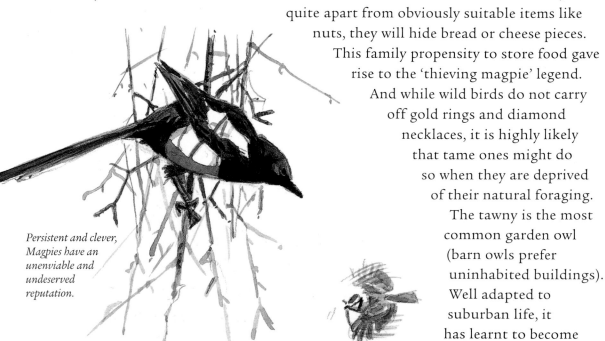

Persistent and clever, Magpies have an unenviable and undeserved reputation.

a bird-catcher, substituting roosting blackbirds, pigeons and sparrows for the more traditional fare of rodents. Possibly Britain's most successful bird of prey, it is also a bird table enthusiast, taking an unwary songbird as it enjoys a late meal of scraps. In fact the proportion of mammal bones in the owl's pellet is dependent on whether it is a country or garden individual: there are more mice and voles in the country, so the owl's diet comprises more small mammals. By contrast, the suburban owl depends a great deal on small birds and is well equipped for catching them. While most birds are fast asleep, the owl makes a living under conditions which to us seem difficult. But he is designed for the job. In poor light conditions he is as much at ease as we are in daylight. He enjoys the same garden, but his is the night-shift, and he brings his senses to bear accordingly.

The eyes have it

Most birds – hunted species – have their eyes placed on either side of the head. This allows for more-or-less all-round vision, giving maximum warning of attack. But the owl's large eyes are in the front of his facial disc and this is significant. Most predators, whether they're insect-chasing swallows or vole-chasing owls, have their eyes placed frontally so that they can see directly ahead and, using their binocular effect, judge distance. Distance is vital information to a hunter. Try closing one eye

Tawny owls are well-suited to suburban life, taking small birds instead of small rodents. During the daytime, however, the roles are reversed and a roosting owl will be pestered mercilessly by even the smallest of birds.

The Owl that, watching in the barn,
Sees the mouse creeping in the corn.
Sits still and shuts his round blue eyes
As if he slept, until he spies
The little beast within his stretch
Then starts, and seizes on the wretch!
***The Barn Owl** Samuel Butler (1612–1680)*

and moving your head from side to side and judge a distance. Then open both and see the improvement. Owls, perching, will bob and bow their heads about, making the most of dim light and measuring the killing swoop.

The owl cannot see in absolute darkness but, after all, that is a rare quality in nature. Owl eyesight is much better than ours, and owl hearing is exceptional, very sensitive to high-frequency sounds, such as the squeaky noises of small rodents as they scamper about the ground. Owl hearing is directional, too, with widespread ear 'receivers' separating stereo left-hand and right-hand sound, so that in the unlikely event of absolute darkness they can pounce on prey using sound information alone. Nocturnal owls often hunt in broad daylight and regularly at dusk and dawn.

Silent flight is another hunting aid for the tawny owl; floating down on whispering engines it surprises its victim. And of course silent flight helps avoid confusion to the owl's listening system: it hears mouse noises uncluttered by the sound of its own wings. They are well-proportioned, spreading the bird's weight over a large surface area. The owl glides easily and leisurely, and has a slow buoyant flight with a slow flap rate. Its feathers are specially modified with a velvety pile, which further damps sound (daytime owls like the little owl do not have this feature). Of course nothing in life is free; that silent flight is slow and energy-intensive, but fortunately the owl doesn't need to fly fast.

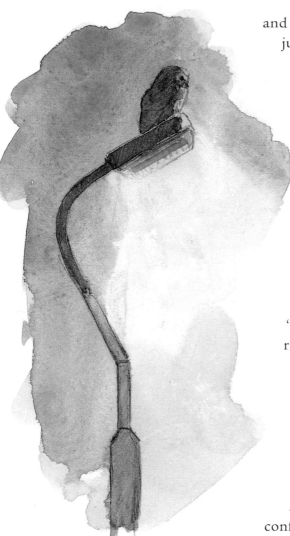

If you are very lucky your nights' sleep may be interrupted by an amorous tawny owl calling from a lamp post outside your bedroom window.

GARDEN OWLS

Tawny and little owls especially take a large number of earthworms and other invertebrate creatures, such as large beetles. In urban and suburban areas tawny owls will prey on small birds, particularly house sparrows and starlings.

Predators and their avoidance

One of the advantages of communal activities, as practised by finches for instance, is that there is safety in numbers, and predators are less likely to take advantage of surprise where many are feeding. For birds have good reason to be apprehensive while foraging at the bird table. However carefully you have sited it, and however effectively you have protected them from land-based predators like cats and weasels, small birds are at risk from potent and persistent enemies, airborne raptors belonging to their own class – owls and hawks.

When a sudden hush descends over your garden, the small birds dashing to disperse in cover, calling only their sharp cries of alarm, there is a predator about. And the small birds are well able to recognize their enemies. A robin will cringe when a sparrowhawk passes, but take no notice at all if a goose flies by. There is good reason for alarm, and the necessary information is programmed into the robin at birth. This innate knowledge tells which creatures to ignore and which to run away from, information that is the result of lessons learnt long ago. Doubtless, the immediate experience of seeing one of your kind killed reinforces the understanding in a powerful manner. And, seeing the encounter from the other viewpoint, it is equally true that the sparrowhawk carries programmed information about suitable prey species. A built-in 'search image' may encourage the sparrowhawk to specialize on blue tits. Sparrowhawks are very efficient at catching small birds. It has been shown that they may take two-and-a-half per cent of a whole chaffinch population in the month of May.

The raptors are well designed for their job as hunter-killers. Sparrowhawks have broad, rounded wings by comparison with the more open-country falcons like peregrines, which have been designed for speed. But sparrowhawks work in amongst the trees and hedgerows, and while they enjoy a fair turn of speed they are also able to engage in fast

Male sparrowhawks go for smaller birds, while the females take thrushes and starlings.

Even a goshawk may visit your garden feeding station, if you're very lucky.

turns and complicated manoeuvres, a useful facility if you're chasing a wildly jinking small bird. Like the other birds of prey, they are able to turn their fourth toe so that it is pointing backwards, allowing a tight grip with two sharp-clawed toes on either side of the victim's body. And the forward motion of the impact as they land on a victim causes the claws to lock automatically and grip fast, a sinister variation on the same mechanism which locks songbirds' feet to their roosting perch when they go to sleep. The bird must make a conscious effort to release its victim.

Sparrowhawks are not the only hunters to enjoy the living bounty of the bird table. Kestrels commonly take house sparrows and young starlings when they get the chance, behaviour that has been most observed in cities. Voles are their preferred diet, and they find good hunting along railway embankments, but if small mammals are scarce they will take many different bird species, and a bird table will become more interesting to them. Perhaps more surprisingly, there are records of kestrels coming to take broken dog biscuits and uncooked bacon rind from an Edinburgh bird table in a cold winter. The fact is that birds of prey are increasingly becoming aware of the potential easy pickings we unintentionally offer to them; no fewer than eight different raptor species have been recorded raiding feeding stations. Apart from sparrowhawk and kestrel, there have been reports of tawny, barn and little owls; merlins; buzzards; and, astonishingly, goshawks. The goshawk was seen taking small birds from a bird table in a Yorkshire garden that adjoined a forestry plantation – typical goshawk habitat. More recently, red kites have taken chicken pieces from a garden lawn.

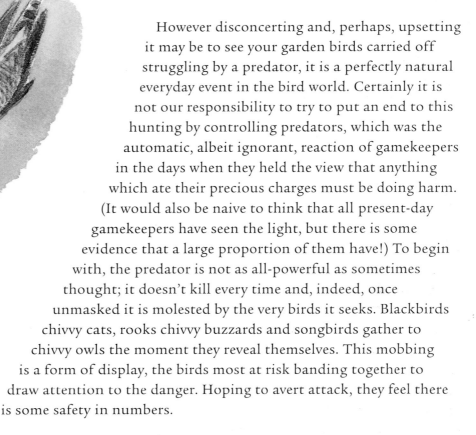

However disconcerting and, perhaps, upsetting it may be to see your garden birds carried off struggling by a predator, it is a perfectly natural everyday event in the bird world. Certainly it is not our responsibility to try to put an end to this hunting by controlling predators, which was the automatic, albeit ignorant, reaction of gamekeepers in the days when they held the view that anything which ate their precious charges must be doing harm. (It would also be naive to think that all present-day gamekeepers have seen the light, but there is some evidence that a large proportion of them have!) To begin with, the predator is not as all-powerful as sometimes thought; it doesn't kill every time and, indeed, once unmasked it is molested by the very birds it seeks. Blackbirds chivvy cats, rooks chivvy buzzards and songbirds gather to chivvy owls the moment they reveal themselves. This mobbing is a form of display, the birds most at risk banding together to draw attention to the danger. Hoping to avert attack, they feel there is some safety in numbers.

Survival of the fittest

The prey taken by a predator represents the slowest/dimmest/weakest/most disabled of its stock, which is improved by this weeding out of less healthy individuals which might have bred and passed on their weakness. It is not in the predator's long-term interest to reduce its prey species. The sparrowhawk wants to ensure that there will be an abundance of sparrows for its progeny to chase. There is a nice parallel here with the behaviour of the foxhunting fraternity which was always concerned to maintain fox numbers in a comfortable balance. Fox hunters and foxes lived together in tolerable harmony.

A bird's life is fraught with natural hazards. After surviving a cold winter, it may get snapped up by a sparrowhawk. If it succeeds in finding a mate and hatching young, there may be a sudden shortage of food and the weaker nestlings may die. The chances of a wild bird living to a ripe old age are remote. So if we are going to invite birds to join us in our gardens there is an obligation on us to try to reduce the hazards, while recognizing the fact that the predator-prey relationship is basically a healthy one, with advantage for both parties.

Falcons are designed for speed. A peregrine dives to attack a pigeon.

Red kites, rapidly becoming more common, have even taken chicken pieces from a garden feeding station. This one was looking for decorative nest material, and was seen thieving smalls from a washing line.

The principal fact, and one that many people find hard to accept, is that on the whole the predator-prey relationship is in the best interest of the species being taken. The hunter catches and despatches the slowest and the sickest of his potential victims, leaving the population stronger and the field free for the best specimens to breed. So the relationship may actually increase the population of the species, which in any case is affected most of all by the amount of food available. Not every attack results in a kill, of course, and every time an animal escapes it emerges just a little wiser, which is good for the species too. In reverse, the number of predators in any given area is determined by the prey available; only the fittest and fastest hunters survive.

Much of the interest in garden-watching consists of observing the fitness of design for purpose in the creatures you see, and surely it is best to learn from the drama, rather than decry it. So I believe in leaving sparrowhawks and crows and cats to get on with it, to their several benefits. And I take pleasure in seeing the speed and power of the sparrowhawk, and try not to think too much about the sparrow. Predators tend to have their senses honed to a fine pitch.

Hunting techniques

Sparrowhawks are seen often enough in gardens, perhaps more often than the commoner kestrel, presumably because the kestrel is adapted for searching out mice and voles in open country. The sparrowhawk is an expert at picking off small birds in flight in the woods and woodland edge, so he is quickly at home in the garden, especially where many small birds congregate at feeding stations. Certainly he is a significant factor in controlling the numbers of sparrows, tits and finches.

Kestrels are at home on motorway verges, long open tracts where mice flourish and sparrowhawks would not feel comfortable. They have taken happily to town life, nesting on the window ledges and crevices of high-rise flats, and feeding on house sparrows. Cities have a lot to offer predators, with a large population of pigeons and sparrows, many of them undernourished and easy prey. Maybe soon we shall be seeing even more peregrines as common city-centre birds, with eyries on the building-cliffsides, and the tidal ebb and flow of traffic to represent the sea below, and with the familiar rock dove/feral pigeon to make them feel at home.

You might want to seal your garden completely from unwelcome predators, but this is more easily said than done. Sparrowhawks and weasels are all part of the natural scene (weasels are adept at raiding nestboxes), but domestic cats and grey squirrels are less acceptable. Ideally, there is no place for them in the bird garden, but you will never keep them out, short of total war. There is some justification for objecting to the way a grey squirrel acts out his predatory role on the small birds in your garden. After all, he is an interloper, indigenous to North America and very ill-advisedly introduced to this country. Grey squirrels eat many eggs, and will even enlarge the entrance hole of a nest box in order to extract and eat the nestlings. In the States they are recognized game animals though there can't be much meat on them. They are a very hardy and successful species, and it's difficult not to have a sneaking regard for them.

Birds will display at a perceived intruder when they see their reflection in glass. This dunnock thinks it is facing competition.

Cats are a problem; if you have both a cat and a bird table you are asking for trouble. What is unfair is to blame the cat for doing something it is designed to do – to hunt. And when it is successful, bringing in sad little bundles of fur or feather to display proudly on the carpet, you must grit your teeth and praise it – and hope that it eats the body, because it compounds the sadness if, having lost its small life, the vole or bird does not even have its goodness recycled by its captor. If you have a cat of your own, at least it serves the useful purpose of discouraging alien cats in defending its territory. And you might like to consider keeping it in for a reasonable and regular period each morning and before dusk, in order to give the birds time to feed.

I have to admit that I like the company of cats and would not care to be without them, but do not try

A correctly fitted collar and bell can reduce cat predation by up to a third, according to research by the RSPB.

to tame your garden birds if you keep a cat. Feed them and make homes for them by all means, but don't encourage them to become too friendly or there will, inevitably, be a tragic outcome.

If you don't want to go as far as installing a wire fence, the best substitute is a thick and prickly hedge. Hawthorn or holly hedges will both in time become fairly impenetrable, although you will always have to watch for secret passageways and block them with bramble or thorn cuttings. The disadvantage of a clipped hedge is that it will not fruit very freely, though, on the other hand, it provides good nesting sites. Allow some of the plants to mature so that a few trees grow out of the hedge to blossom and fruit. Holly is particularly good, because the dead leaves cover the soil underneath with spiny points which may deter cats, weasels and such like.

Rats have to be taken seriously. They climb well, even shinning up trees and hedges to search for eggs and young birds, and a good bird garden is also an attractive rat garden. So food should not be left on the ground at night, and windfalls too should be cleared away every evening: they can become part of the winter bird table menu.

Keep the cats away

- Place feeders high off the ground but away from surfaces from which a cat could jump.
- Place spiny plants (such as holly) or an uncomfortable surface around the base of the feeding station to prevent cats sitting underneath it.
- Place an upturned tin or cone underneath the table to prevent cats from climbing the post (squirrel baffles are already commercially available).
- Make the table-stand slippery using a metal post, or plastic bottles around non-metal posts.
- Plant wildlife-friendly vegetation, such as prickly bushes and thick climbers in the garden to provide secure cover for birds. These should be close enough to where birds feed to provide cover, but not so close that cats can use it to stalk birds.
- Cat deterrents such as ultrasonic devices and strong-smelling repellents are readily available. The effectiveness of these is probably variable, and there is little scientific evidence of their effectiveness. Some are also quite expensive. However, many people tell me that they have achieved good results with some of these techniques, so it must remain a matter of individual choice whether to use them or not.

Are cats causing bird declines?

Despite the large numbers of birds killed, there is no scientific evidence that predation by cats in gardens is having any impact on bird populations UK wide. This may be surprising, but many millions of birds die naturally every year, mainly through starvation, disease, or other forms of predation. There is evidence that cats tend to take weak or sickly birds. We also know that of the millions of baby birds hatched each year, most will die before they reach breeding age. This is also quite natural, and each pair needs only to rear two young that survive to breeding age to replace themselves and maintain the population. It is likely that most of the birds killed by cats would have died anyway from other causes before the next breeding season, so cats are unlikely to have a major impact on populations. If their predation was additional to these other causes of mortality, this might have a serious impact on bird populations.

Keeping things clean

It is important to keep a bird table clean because there is an ever-present danger of bacterial infection when bird droppings accumulate. Salmonella kills birds and some infections are also transmissible to humans. Use a five per cent bleach solution or Ark Klens (see Jacobi Jayne page 180 for suppliers) and clean regularly. Boiling water is an alternative way of doing the job.

Move the table occasionally to discourage a build-up of the potentially dangerous droppings. Do not allow uneaten food to accumulate. And a warning – don't overfeed your birds. It doesn't make sense to provide great mounds of food, attracting quantities of birds and increasing the risk of salmonellosis and tuberculosis, both of which are common bacterial infections in wild birds. The object should be to provide a welcome supplement, but not so much as to induce dependence on bird table food at the expense of active foraging for a diversity of wild seeds, grasses and insects in a natural manner.

Regular cleaning and disinfecting of bird tables, bird baths and hanging feeders is an important part of good hygiene practice when feeding garden birds. Alongside these measures, it is important not to provide more food than birds need. Ideally, bird tables should be swept clean each day to remove droppings and any uneaten food.

For information on pest control without poison, contact Garden Organic, formerly the Henry Doubleday Research Association (address page 179).

Garden birdwatch schemes

Years ago the BTO launched the Garden Bird Feeding Survey with the main aim of determining which species make use of gardens at different times of year; what range of foods is provided in gardens and which are the preferred ones. Since then bird gardeners and other householders – sometimes with little more than a backyard or a window box – have contributed to the survey from all parts of the country. In the first ten years of the survey alone, 199 different species were recorded in gardens for which observations were sent in! The mind boggles at the gardens that produced wigeon, red kite,

The musical song thrush suffered a serious decline in numbers which began in the mid 1970s, but this seems to have levelled and may even have reversed.

Red kites collect nest twigs to 'improve' an old buzzard or raven nest, which they take over.

TOP 12 GARDEN BIRDS

Blackbird
Blue tit
Chaffinch
Robin
Collared dove
Dunnock
Great tit
Greenfinch
Coal tit
House sparrow
Magpie
Starling

Bewick's swan and an American blue jay. What is proved beyond dispute by the survey is the enormous range of species which do, from time to time, make use of our gardens and the important part which all these gardens play for birds in our ever-shrinking countryside. Another important fact disclosed is the extent to which the number and variety of birds differs from year to year depending on the severity of the winter. The conclusion is clear: garden bird feeding in winter is a major contributor to the survival of many of our individual birds.

The survey now seeks to attract garden enthusiasts all of whom are supplied with special recording forms and asked to record details of the use which different birds make of the garden. The 'new' Garden Bird Survey not only produces a lot more detail about birds' feeding preferences in gardens but also provides important information on the extent to which different breeding species use our gardens for nesting in different parts of the country. Special emphasis too is placed on one or two species that are currently declining on farmland and that make some use of gardens, for example, the linnet and tree sparrow, and the magpie, which has increased rapidly in suburban gardens in recent years and is accused by some of undue depletion of garden songbirds.

One question the bird gardener asks is: 'What are the commonest garden species?' The results of the years of surveying so far undertaken can give this answer with authority. Although the relative position of each of the commonest species may vary a little from one year to the next, the Top 12 are usually as listed left.

In most years these 12 are followed, a few percentage points behind, by wren, black-headed gull and pied wagtail. Not surprisingly, with all this bounty of feathered food on hand, the sparrowhawk comes in around 20th place. Whether or not you take part in the survey, keep a list of all the species you see in your garden: it will surprise you.

The BTO/CJ Garden BirdWatch Scheme is the largest year-round study of how birds use gardens across Britain and Ireland. Valuable information gained is then used to help declining species such as house sparrow, song thrush and starling.

The strength of the scheme is in its participants, so why not join over 16,500 people and make your garden count towards bird conservation. All you need do is keep simple weekly records of your garden visitors. You can even enter and view your results over the Internet.

Write for details to Garden BirdWatch at the British Trust for Ornithology (address on page 178). They will be pleased to hear from you, whether you have a hectare (2 acre) spread in Sunningdale, a backyard in Halifax or a lighthouse compound in the Irish Sea.

Finally, don't be discouraged if, after all your efforts, birds don't immediately flock to your feast. It takes them time to adjust to a new feeding opportunity, as you will find if you move a familiar device, or paint something a new colour. Or perhaps there is a welcome abundance of natural food nearby, which will of course be more attractive, nutritious and generally health-promoting than anything you may have provided. In any event, having fed the resident birds through the winter, you will have ensured that they have a good start for the coming breeding season, and providing good nesting sites is the object of our attention in the next chapter.

Hawfinches may become surprisingly tame in well-timbered suburban areas. They carry the most powerful of all finch beaks, a real nutcracker that can cope with even cherry or plum stones in order to get at the kernel.

Nestboxes

A wide variety of suitable nesting sites will of course make a garden even more desirable to birds. While winter visiting thrushes are returning to their Scandinavian breeding grounds, resident blackbirds, robins and finches are establishing territories and being joined by spring migrants such as warblers and martins. As well as ensuring there are lots of natural nest sites, we can give them even more options by providing a few nestboxes.

History of nestboxes

Man-made nest sites have a long history, but originally their purpose was almost entirely in connection with the food potential of the species involved.

Pigeon houses

It seems likely that pigeons were the first birds to be domesticated, by way of artificial nesting ledges, which encouraged the truly wild coastal rock doves to breed in places where the keeper could harvest his share of the fat squabs. Pigeons were ideal candidates for domestication, with undemanding food requirements, an easily satisfied specification for nesting places, an easy-going disposition and tolerance of humans. Above all, they had the astonishing ability to rear as many as ten clutches in a year, nourishing a pair of well-grown squabs while they incubated the next pair of eggs in the production line.

The pigeons' technique for feeding young, even in the depths of winter, relies on their ability to produce 'pigeon milk' from their crops. The formation of this food is controlled by a hormone, prolactin, which is produced by both cock and hen in the last days of incubation. Thus, they are ready to ensure a protein supply to the newly hatched chicks for the first few days, till they are strong enough to eat at least a little solid food. After a few days the milk is supplemented with choice pieces of soft food. As time goes by hormonal cueing changes the ratio, so that the young get less and less milk.

Pigeons as symbols and food

Probably the first of these birds to be domesticated was in the eastern Mediterranean. There are images of the pigeon in art dating back to 3100BC, and certainly the birds were used as a source of food in Egypt before 2600BC. In early cultures pigeons were sacred birds, associated with Astarte, the Hindu goddess of fertility and fruitfulness. In India, as sacred birds, they were allowed to colonize buildings and temples without hindrance and without being managed for food. In classical Greece they were associated with Aphrodite, as love symbols. The Romans linked pigeons with Venus in the same way, but prudently took advantage of their culinary qualities, as well as using them for messengers. Indeed, as Pliny the Elder (AD23–70) wrote in *Natural History:* 'Many persons have quite a mania for pigeons – building towers for them on the top of their roofs, and taking pleasure in relating the pedigree and noble origin of each.'

As enthusiastic pigeon fanciers, the Romans must have built pigeon cities, columbaria, in England. Whether the Saxons did so is not clear, but the word 'cote' refers in part to a bird house, and 'culver', though less widespread, probably refers to the woodpigeon and gave rise to 'culver house'. 'Doocot' is clear enough in its meaning and, indeed, the Scots have cultured pigeons for a very long time. Near the coastal village of East Wemyss, in Fife, there are two caves with dozens of man-made ledge-holes cut out of the walls and the artificially enlarged roof, clearly designed to encourage rock doves. Carvings on the walls date back to the early Bronze Age, but are mainly Pictish (AD400–900). Sadly, the archaeologists are as yet unable to date the pigeon holes, so we can't say whether the Picts farmed the pigeons or whether the practice was first associated with the later development of the nearby 14th-century castles of Wemyss and Macduff.

A typical pigeon house in the south-west of France.

Medieval pigeons

More widespread rearing of semi-domesticated pigeons for fresh meat, especially in winter, began in Britain with the Norman invasion, when the conquerors introduced the science of the 'colombier'. No 12th-century castle was complete without its rows of pigeon holes, carefully built into a turret or high place, sheltered and south facing, with the enormous advantage that the birds foraged far and wide for their own food and did not require sustenance from a besieged garrison's meagre supplies. Soon the gentle pigeon became associated not only with warlike places, but the substantial stone-built dovecot became an important part of any manor house or monastery.

On the wild Gower coast of South Wales, a natural cliff fissure was enclosed at some time in the 13th or 14th century to form a hollow pigeon buttress, known as the 'culver hole'. There were ramps giving access for the keeper, and three elegant slits making entrances for the birds – yet another arrangement designed to tempt wild rock doves to nest so that the occupants of a nearby castle could take a proportion of the squabs. The culver hole was rebuilt in the 15th century and still stands today, an astonishing structure which reminds us of the one-time importance of pigeon culture.

By the late 13th century a medieval bishop on his travels would expect a high standard of victualling, the dinner table liberally provided with fresh meat even in the dark days of winter. On tour, his chaplain would record disbursements for wine, beer, beef and so on. One note tells of His Lordship's purchase of '2 carcasses of beef, 9s 4d, 25 geese 5s 2d, 24 pigeons 8d'. So along with the fish pond and the rabbit warren and the duck decoy, the dovecot was an important item in medieval animal architecture. Conradus Heresbachius, in his *Husbandrie*, 1577, wrote: 'it behoveth especially to have good care for breeding of pigeons, as well for the great commoditie they yeelde to the kitchin, as for the profit and yearely revenue that they yeelde (if there be good store of corne seedes) in the market'.

The interior of a classic Norman 'colombier' would have 500 pigeon-holes, each accessible by way of a ladder fixed to a central 'potence'.

Pigeon house design

The pigeon house was always carefully sited, to provide protection from prevailing winds. The Norman design involved a circular building with walls 1m thick (no windows), tapering at the very top of the roof to a 'lantern', which gave entrance for the birds. A door at ground level admitted the pigeon keeper. Inside, the walls were pierced with row after row of pigeon-holes, 'three handfulles in length, and ledged from hole to hole for them to walke upon'. An ingenious device called a potence allowed the keeper to reach any nest at any height by means of a ladder which rotated on a central pillar passing within a couple of inches of the wall as it was pushed around. The interior was dim, to the liking of the pigeons, and each pair of birds had a double nest site because before one set of squabs was ready to leave the nest the hen might well have laid her next clutch of eggs.

Traditional pigeon-houses became redundant in the 19th century – nowadays they are represented by ornamental garden versions.

As time went by, the pigeon houses improved in design and, especially in areas lacking local stone, they would be built of timber or brick and set on pillars. This had the great benefit of affording protection from predators such as rats, cats, weasels and squirrels. Hawks and owls were also a problem. Heresbachius wrote in 1577: 'I found of late in myne own Dovehouse, an Owle sitting solemnly in the Nest upon her Egges in the middest of all the Pigions, by reason of the thickness of his feathers, yet will creep in at as little a place as the Pigion will; so small and little is their bodies, though they be bombased with feathers'.

Up on the roof, the pigeons would have a promenading area, sheltered from cold winds and facing south to catch the best of the sun. Under the whole structure there might well be room for a stable or cow house, giving the benefit of extra warmth in winter, to encourage breeding. Everything was done to aid these *'wondrous fruitfull'* birds. Each year the best of the early squabs were carefully selected for breeding. The less satisfactory – 'unfruitefull and naughtie coloured, and otherwise faulty' – quickly found themselves being fattened for the table.

Pigeons – additional uses

For those whose status ran to it, pigeons offered a far better return than lowly sparrows. By the end of the 17th century, John Smyth could write of the Berkeley family of Gloucestershire: 'In each manor and almost upon each farm house he had a pigeon house, and in divers manors two. And in Hame and a few other (where his dwelling houses were) three: from each house he drew yearly great numbers. As 1300, 1200, 1000, 850, 700, 650 from an house. And from Hame one year 2151 young pigeons.' These squabs must have represented an important source of revenue, fetching 2d a dozen, a worthwhile sum at that time.

Not only the fat squabs had value: the plentiful droppings which piled conveniently on the dovecot floor were rich in nitrogen and minerals. 'Doves dung is best of all others for Plants and Seeds, and may be scattered when anything is sown together with the seed, or at any time afterwards. One basketful thereof is worth a cartload of sheep's dung. Our countrymen also are wont to sow Doves dung together with their grain' (*The Ornithology* Francis Willughby, 1678). In Persia the dung was used to fertilize melon fields; in south-west France, where it was used in vineyards, dovecots were often kept as much for the value of the dung as the squabs.

Dung was also used in the tannery process, in removing hair from the hides, and as part of the process in making saltpetre for gunpowder. In addition it was used as a specific against the plague and the palsy. 'The flesh of young pigeons is restorative and useful to recruit the strength of such as are getting up or newly recovered from some great sickness' (Willughby, 1678).

But the privileged aspects of pigeon-keeping involved social injustice. While they might be owned by the lord of the manor, the birds thought nothing of eating the peasant's or yeoman's corn. And lawyers offered no redress, as the jurist, John Selden, wrote in the early 17th century: 'Some men may make it a case of conscience whether a man may have a pigeon house, because his pigeons eat other folks' corn. But there is no such thing as conscience in the business: the matter is, whether he be a man of such quality that the state allows him to have a dove house; if so, there is an end of the business: his pigeons have a right to eat where they please themselves.'

Plump pigeon squabs were a valuable source of year-round meat.

So the yeomen and tenant farmers gradually tore the shaky fabric of this law to pieces, building their own version of the free-standing pigeon houses, opening neat rows of nest-holes along the walls of their barns and farmhouses. The pigeon house came to an end when new agricultural practices made it possible to sustain more cattle and sheep through the winter months, thus making butcher's meat available throughout the year.

Rock doves

Most pigeon houses now lie derelict, while their inhabitants' descendants make a living in our city streets or in the sport of racing. Their truly wild ancestors have fared little better. Sadly, the wild coastal rock dove is becoming increasingly rare. A number of small populations of the pure-bred birds exist, confined to the north and west coasts, and Scottish and Irish islands. Apart from those far flung Celtic outposts of pure-bred birds, rock doves are now represented only by the cliffside colonies of racing pigeons that have given up the sport, and by the ubiquitous street pigeon, which itself represents a hopeless mix of long-ago-escaped dovecot stock and more recent racing pigeon dropouts. Mixed or not, all domestic pigeons owe common ancestry to the rock dove.

All domestic pigeons – racers, dovecot, messenger and fancy breeds – are descended from the rock dove, now extremely rare as a British wild bird.

Sparrow flasks

The peasants made do with clay pots set up to attract sparrows and starlings, from which they took the first broods of nestlings when they were fat enough to eat. This procedure, using wooden cistulae (flasks), was used in Silesia; and practised in Holland, with unglazed earthenware pots, in the late Middle Ages. In France they hung similar earthenware pots under the eaves of the houses in the region of Toulouse. When the Dutchmen came to drain the East Anglian fenlands in the mid-17th century they brought the practice with them. Before this time sparrows had been paid as part of the rent, according to Norfolk rent books dating back to 1533, so one assumes the locals already had some knowledge of the technique.

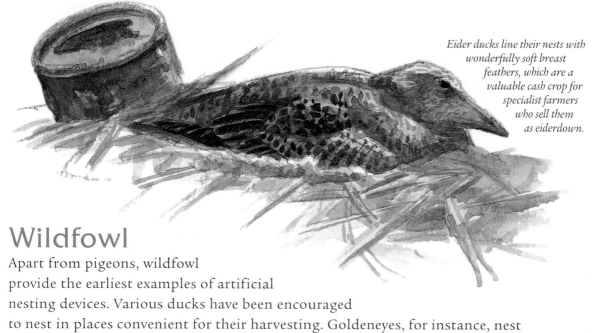

Eider ducks line their nests with wonderfully soft breast feathers, which are a valuable cash crop for specialist farmers who sell them as eiderdown.

Wildfowl

Apart from pigeons, wildfowl provide the earliest examples of artificial nesting devices. Various ducks have been encouraged to nest in places convenient for their harvesting. Goldeneyes, for instance, nest naturally in tree holes or tree stumps, and by the late Middle Ages the Lapps were improving natural sites to attract them as a food source, mainly for the eggs.

Not long after the Viking colonization of Iceland, coastal farmers realized the special qualities of the breast feathers of eiders. Lining the nest with its breast feathers, this sea duck arranges an eider-down quilt to cover and retain the warmth of the eggs if she leaves the nest for any reason. By the cunning provision of carefully placed sticks and stones (the birds like to nest against something), the farmers created conditions that suited the ducks and so encouraged the formation of colonies in places that were convenient for the down collector. The practice is still followed today, and farmers go to great lengths to please their worker birds, which are fortunately fairly tame. They provide music in the form of wind-activated instruments and hang coloured ribbons in string, both of which are supposed to act as added attractions. Some of the eider colonies are

Goldeneye ducklings have to jump out of their nests, usually in holes in trees.

large, with anything up to ten thousand pairs nesting. The down is taken twice in each season, once just before the eggs hatch, when the lining is removed, and again after the young have left the nest. The down, which is carefully cleansed of any dirt and grass or large feathers, represents a substantial income to the farmers. They have a vested interest, of course, in making sure the eiders breed successfully and continue to patronize the facilities so carefully provided. Both farmers and birds benefit from the arrangement.

Eiders are one of the most numerous duck species in the world, their winter population in Europe totalling more than two million. Since the mid-19th century their range has been expanding and we now have sizeable breeding numbers in Scotland – perhaps one day we shall see the birth of a new British industry. In passing, we should note that the same basic technique pioneered for attracting eiders to nest, that is the provision of suitably shaped sticks or stones in a featureless landscape, has been used by egg collectors wanting to plunder the eggs of greenshanks, whose moorland nests are notoriously difficult to find. (It is, of course, illegal to take any eggs.)

Mallards

Doubtless mallard ducks, and others, have been provided with convenient nest sites (convenient for the plunderer, that is) in Britain for centuries, but it is not easy to find evidence of them. Decoys, which date back to somewhere round the 13th century, were set to live-trap migrant wildfowl in winter, and this practice certainly led to a small-scale provision of nesting facilities in the breeding season. Perhaps the first record of duck boxes in Britain comes from the diarist John Evelyn, a friend of Samuel Pepys and a mine of information on the times of Charles II. In his diary entry for 9 February 1665, he writes: 'I went to St James's Park ... at this time stored with numerous flocks of ... wildfowl, breeding about the Decoy, which for being so near so great a city, and among such a concourse of soldiers and people, is a singular and diverting thing ... There were withy-potts or nests for wildfowl to lay their eggs in, a little above the surface of the water.' The designer of the decoy, incidentally, Sydrach Hileus, was a Dutchman who had been brought over especially to do the job.

In the past, landowners created nesting islands at convenient coastal locations to encourage black-headed gulls to lay marketable eggs.

Nestboxes for pleasure

So far, all these examples of artificial nestboxes or man-assisted nesting places have had a culinary or commercial significance. Perhaps the first known record of birds attracted to an artificial nest site purely for aesthetic reasons, was that of Gilbert White's brother Thomas, who, as Gilbert recorded in his journal for 5 June 1782, nailed up several large scallop shells under the eaves of his house at South Lambeth, to see if the house martins would build in them. 'These conveniences had not been fixed half an hour before several pairs settled upon them; and expressing great complacency began to build immediately. The shells were nailed on horizontally with the hollow side upwards; and if you choose to try it for yourself, should have a hole drilled in their bottoms to let off moisture from driving rains.'

Charles Waterton, whose pioneer wildlife reserve was described earlier, developed the use of nestboxes in the early 19th century, as also did the other pioneer ornithologist, J.F. Dovaston. Unfortunately, although we know Dovaston used boxes in connection with his experiments, which may have been the first to consider the principles of territory in bird behaviour, he left precious little published information on them – a terrible lesson for all amateur scientists who fail to record their findings! Waterton wrote fully, so we know for example that he made (possibly in 1816) an artificial sand quarry with 50 deep holes in a sheltered and sunny part of the grounds of Walton Park. And we can imagine his pleasure and delight when, the very next summer, sand martins arrived in his reserve for the first time to found a thriving colony. (A similar experiment, equally successful, may be seen today by the pond near the visitor centre at the RSPB's Minsmere reserve in Suffolk. Try it for yourself: in a sandbank, create a 50mm (2in) tunnel to a nest chamber!)

Sand martins are easily encouraged to colonize suitable man-made quarry holes.

Owl houses

Waterton improved hollow trees to make them more attractive for tawny owls, and developed a barn owl house 'on the ruin of the old gateway, against which, tradition says, the waves of the lake have dashed for the best part of a thousand years. I made a place with stone and mortar, about four feet square, and fixed a thick oaken stick firmly into it. In about a month or so after it was finished, a pair of Barn Owls came and took up their abode in it. I threatened to strangle the keeper if ever, after this, he molested either the old birds or their young ones.' Waterton was so delighted with his success that he subsequently built four other owl establishments, all of which were occupied. He also built a tower for starlings, rather in the style of a garden dovecot. Its stone pillar, smooth and vertical, was surmounted by a flat circular stone with sharply sloping edges, measures all designed to discourage rats. On top of this he placed a circular stone house, with conical roof, each course of stones having some loose ones, channelled to allow inspection access to the nest chamber behind. Although Waterton was regarded as little more than an eccentric in his own time, many of his ideas sowed the seeds of a whole new attitude to wildlife which were to bear a great deal of fruit later.

Woodland boxes

By 1897, 20 species were known to have bred in boxes or platforms of some kind in Britain. But the pioneer of large-scale bird manipulation by the use of nestboxes was the Baron von Berlepsch. His primary interest was the control of insect pests in his woodland, but there is no doubt he had aesthetic considerations firmly in mind. His main interest was in methods of increasing woodland bird populations in areas where foresters were intolerant of trees past their maturity, and nestboxes played an important part in his operations. Before his time, these devices had been relatively ineffective. He brought a cold and logical eye to the requirements and pursued them with relentless efficiency, pouring scorn on bird 'inventions' which had suffered failures in the past for not being

Pied flycatchers readily use 'man-made holes in trees'. They prefer nestboxes to the real thing in some woods.

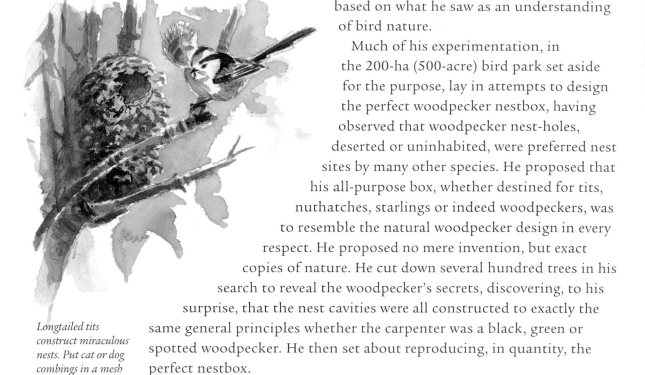

Longtailed tits construct miraculous nests. Put cat or dog combings in a mesh cage and they will be truly grateful.

based on what he saw as an understanding of bird nature.

Much of his experimentation, in the 200-ha (500-acre) bird park set aside for the purpose, lay in attempts to design the perfect woodpecker nestbox, having observed that woodpecker nest-holes, deserted or uninhabited, were preferred nest sites by many other species. He proposed that his all-purpose box, whether destined for tits, nuthatches, starlings or indeed woodpeckers, was to resemble the natural woodpecker design in every respect. He proposed no mere invention, but exact copies of nature. He cut down several hundred trees in his search to reveal the woodpecker's secrets, discovering, to his surprise, that the nest cavities were all constructed to exactly the same general principles whether the carpenter was a black, green or spotted woodpecker. He then set about reproducing, in quantity, the perfect nestbox.

In fact, Berlepsch went too far, since as we know only too well, birds will occupy boxes of almost any shape, size or colour provided they offer certain fundamental design advantages – most particularly that the entrance hole is of the correct size. But, after measuring hundreds of natural woodpecker excavations, he specified that his boxes should reproduce those measurements precisely. He wouldn't allow tin guards around the entrance holes (to discourage great spotted woodpeckers from taking over from tits) on the grounds that they destroyed the natural appearance of the boxes ('their chief merit'), and said that such 'guarded' boxes were never occupied, a claim that seems nonsensical today.

Nesting success

In one wood Berlepsch set up 2000 of his boxes, and claimed 90 per cent occupancy; and in his bird park, he had 300 boxes occupied by birds of 14 species. But although he went to some length to provide additional food for his birds in order to sustain an abundant population, it is not clear that he fully understood the overriding importance that food availability has in controlling bird numbers. He believed that the provision of nest sites was paramount. Nevertheless, he was the first to make nestboxing popular; his boxes were successful, they were manufactured in large quantities both in Germany and – under licence – abroad. In the early years of the 20th century the newly formed RSPB offered them in various sizes, for sale at prices varying from 1s 6d to 5s 6d. Berlepsch left his mark on the commercial world of nestbox production, and it was years before cheaper, less natural, but equally effective, versions were on the market. In one major respect Berlepsch strayed off the path of righteousness: he believed firmly in controlling predators, creatures he called the enemies of his birds. His blacklist included cats, squirrels, weasels, martens, polecats, house and tree sparrows, shrikes, sparrowhawks, goshawks, jays, magpies and carrion crows – for whose demise he offered rewards.

From Berlepsch's time, boxes were used systematically by scientists engaged in population studies. In the case of the pied flycatcher, which takes to nestboxes as ducks take to water, whole woodland populations have preferred the artificial sites to anything a tree has to offer, and tens of thousands of birds have been ringed in research directed towards analysing their life-style. A great deal of work has also been done on the nesting behaviour of blue and great tits, and of tawny owls.

Improving natural nest sites

It is the diversity of food offered by a mature garden which induces so many birds either to make a permanent home in the garden, or to return year after year as summer visitors. The availability of nest-sites is important, of course, but far and away the greatest attraction is a food supply that will make it possible to rear youngsters. This is why birds rarely have the temerity to nest in the winter; it can happen, but the odds against success are high and the evolutionary process soon stops it. Birds born during a food shortage do not survive to perpetuate the mistake. Natural selection determines the breeding season, as everything else. In spring and summer there is more plant material, more insect life, more warmth, more light and longer days, so that is when courtship comes to a climax.

A window ledge is an unusual nest site for a blackbird. This is the kind of site chosen by a kittiwake or a peregrine in different circumstances.

Small birds lay eggs in time for the nestlings to benefit from the peak caterpillar population of May and June. Sparrowhawks lay a little later, so that they benefit from the peak small-bird population! Second broods are less likely to succeed because they have missed the insect peak. Pigseons breed almost through the year, but that is because they feed their young on 'milk', which they can manufacture from whatever foods are available at the time.

Choosing a plot

Choosing the building site will be part of the courtship activity, and may be decided long before construction work begins. Resident birds may have spent the winter searching for a plot, but summer visitors have less time to waste. They may select a site and begin construction on the same day. Either way the hole-nesters like tits have a more difficult task, as suitable holes are not easy to find, even if they do grow on trees! Even so, a cock great tit may find several sites and take his hen on a tour of inspection. She makes the final choice, displaying her pleasure with shivering wing movements. A particular site may be attractive to more than one pair of birds. Blue tits may build a nest and lay eggs, only to be evicted by tree sparrows which actually build another nest on top of the existing one, eggs and all, and proceed to lay their own clutch.

There is no stranger sight in spring than a housing estate with a clockwork starling on nearly every rooftop or gutter, flapping his wings mechanically, singing his head off.

Building materials, as in all the most harmonious houses, will be found nearby, and will depend on the local vegetation and on the secondhand market. It is in the early stages of nest building that you have your best chance of identifying the site, because you will see birds struggling to get airborne with sticks

Urban sparrows

It has been estimated that suburban and urban habitats now support about 50 per cent of the British house sparrow population. The house sparrow has long been associated with human settlement. The decline of the horse as a means of transport in the 1920s meant that the sparrow population also declined in cities and towns. More recently, modern building practices may have contributed to its decline. PVC fascia boards and roof furnishings, and the replacement of thatched roofs by tiles and slates have reduced the number of nesting sites. There may be other causes: increased predation by cats; pollution from unleaded petrol; more use of garden pesticides.

and grass, before flying to the works. Much material may be wasted as the main timbers fall to the ground, to be left there while the bird goes off to find more. But once the framework is stable the bird will shape the cup by moving around, both ways, and working with its breast and feet. Grasses and mosses will be packed tight, and the bill will be used to work in odd strands. After the main structure is finished, another layer may be added; for instance, a blackbird will have a mud course. Swallows and house martins also need mud, so in a dry spell remember to throw a pail of water on some bare earth for them – mud-pie making is hard work without water.

Birds will be grateful for suitable nestmaking material offered in early spring.

Tie-on plant labels are a favourite nest material, though goldfinches actually untie the string, which involves quite intricate manipulative behaviour. One jackdaw's nest held 67 plant labels. Polystyrene chippings are popular, perhaps providing extra warmth and insulation – 1,500 were solemnly counted in the nest of one long-tailed tit. Pigeons go for sterner stuff, like stainless-steel wire. Short lengths of wire are not so very different from twigs, so there is really no behavioural significance in any of these odd uses of man-made materials. Birds just use available resources to the best advantage.

Birds may build several nests. One mistle thrush actually started five, but finished two. The problem was that it was building on top of a pillar at a power station, and there wasn't just one pillar but dozens of them, regularly spaced 6m (20ft) apart in a block. The unfortunate bird became disorientated by the multiplicity of identical sites, and didn't always land on the same pillar.

Nest building is part of a routine, and it has to start at the beginning, with the establishment of a territory and with courtship. Without this stimulus, an unmated hen is very unlikely to build a nest and lay eggs, although it does happen. (The domesticated chicken is an example, but this is a bird that has been painstakingly selected for just this function.) Cock wrens build nests for a pastime, and in other countries the cock weaver birds build half a nest from which to display, before completing the job. But normally first things come first, and there's no nest without a partnership.

Birds are easily disturbed and may abandon the project in the early stages of nest building. Many desert if they are hassled. If you must go and look, do it in an ordinary, everyday sort of manner. Walk quietly up to the nest, passing and returning to it, talking as you go, and generally act like the blundering mammal that you are. At all costs avoid a slow approach with a direct gazing stare. The birds will resent this abnormal and inexplicable behaviour. Do not poke a finger into a hole-nest. Wrens, for instance, sit very tight, but will readily desert if you start touching them. Do not cut away leaves or twigs to see the nest more easily; this will simply be an invitation to the nearest predator. Photographers are the greatest menace in this respect. For my part I do not search for nests and I prefer to leave birds to get on with the job without my interference, and that goes as far as not getting in the way when magpies are at their dirty work of egg-thieving, or woodpeckers are baby-snatching. If a bird deserts the nest, it has to start again elsewhere from the beginning. It takes an intelligent mammal, like a fox or you or me, to have the sense to pick up the juveniles and carry them off elsewhere to start a new life!

Tree improvements

Much woodland is managed for maximum timber production and decaying trees are not tolerated. So there is a chance for the bird gardener to redress the balance if he allows a dying tree to live out its time. It will give interest out of all proportion to its cash value.

It may be that you already have some old trees – fruit trees, perhaps – which have begun to decay in a manner attractive to birds. If not, you might consider introducing some holes into a decaying tree with a brace and bit. Start some promising holes of about 32mm (1¼in) diameter and a woodpecker may finish the job. If the woodpecker gives up, a nuthatch may take over and plaster the entrance hole with mud to suit its own

Robins choose to nest in the open, but the site is carefully chosen for maximum concealment from prying eyes. Put an old teapot out in the ivy, you never know. Make sure the spout points down for drainage.

preference. Or, you might try
importing an old tree or tree trunk,
complete with holes, and setting it
up in a secluded position. You
may end up with a pair of
starlings if you are lucky. They
are entertaining vocalists and
remarkable mimics. We once had
one that gave a first-class rendering
of a hen that had just laid an egg, but
the climax of its repertoire was a beautiful
pussy-cat's miaow.

The nuthatch makes the entrance hole to its nest a snug fit by plastering it with mud.

When you have finished working on trees, you
might turn your attention to the walls of your
house and outbuildings. Quite often it is possible
to enlarge cracks so that there is the 29mm (1⅛in)
necessary for a tit to squeeze through. I am not
suggesting you tear your house apart just for a few birds, but
you will find plenty of likely and safe places if you look around, armed
with a strong auger or jemmy. Try drilling some discreet 32mm (1¼in)
holes in your garage doors. Make one entrance up near the roof and
swallows may colonize the joists, although you will need to protect
your car from the droppings.

If you are building a garden wall, do not overdo the pointing; leave
one or two gaps and you may attract a pied wagtail. Even grey wagtails
take freely to man-provided nest sites in culverts and bridge stonework.
The height of the holes and cavities is not vitally important, although
round about the 1.5m (5ft) mark is probably ideal. With a desirable
site, birds will not be too choosy. Robins have nested at ground level
and great tits as high as 7.2m (24ft), although these are exceptional
instances. The holes should, however, be in a sheltered position and
facing somewhere within an arc drawn from north through east to
south-east. Hot sun is bad, and so is an entrance facing into a cold
wind. Extremes of temperature can easily kill young nestlings.

An ancient, disintegrating stone wall is an asset to cherish and so is
an old garden shed. The wall may be a haven for tits, nuthatches and
wagtails, and the shed may be a thriving bird slum in no time at all if
you develop it a little. Shelves around the walls and under the roof at
different heights could provide homes for swallows, blackbirds and

Aquatic birds like black-throated divers often choose to find a nest place in the most remote and undisturbed areas. These are birds of the wildest Hebrides and north-east Scotland. The RSPB has helped them in recent years with the construction of artificial nest rafts.

robins. A bundle of pea sticks in a corner may make a home for a wren. Leave an old tweed coat hanging up with a wide pocket gaping open for a robin. Keep the floor clear, though, to discourage rats. If necessary put a rat-trap tunnel against the walls, but see that it does not let in light and attract ground birds. Make sure there is a good entrance hole somewhere, in case a bird is locked in by mistake.

Sheds and roof spaces

On the outside of the shed, grow a jungle of creeping ivy and honeysuckle, for it may well entice a robin to build. Hide a half-coconut (with a hole in the bottom of the cup for drainage) in the creeper for a possible spotted flycatcher. Try excavating a nest cavity in the middle of a brushwood bundle and lean it against an outside wall. And lean an old plank against the dampest, darkest wall to make a haven for snails, and farm them on behalf of the thrushes.

If all is well, your roof-space will provide dry warm quarters for yet another community. More bugs and spiders will reside here, starlings and sparrows will find their way in through incredibly small entrance holes and import grasses to improve the facilities. Even barn owls may nest if you provide a decent-sized entrance and an apple box for a nursery. Deep crevices and ledges may entice swifts to come in from their aerial outdoor life, but they tend to go for old buildings, tall towers and tall houses, anywhere where there's a dark almost inaccessible hole. Their nest will be made of material collected in the air itself – flying straws, feathers, cotton – all gummed together with saliva. In the romantic Far East, cousins of swifts – cave swiftlets – provide the salivary secretion that spawns birdsnest soup. Presumably there's no reason why we shouldn't eat British swifts' birdsnest soup, the saliva must be much the same. But it is well and truly mixed with feathers and other junk and would need a lot of cleaning.

Man-made nest sites

The traditional back-garden nestbox is a kettle for a robin, stuck 1.5m (5ft) up in the fork of a tree. The kettle should be at least quart size, and the spout should point down so that the rainwater can drain away. As an encouragement, prime the nest with some dead leaves or a plaited circle of straw.

The most unusual man-made nest site I ever saw was a birdcage, hanging high up on a cob wall in the village of Middle Wallop in Hampshire. It turned out that a hoopoe had reared young in a perfectly normal cavity-site in the wall, but one of the nestlings had fallen out of the hole a bit too soon. The villagers had hoisted up the birdcage, and left the door open, installing the unfortunate young bird inside. Incredibly, the adult hoopoe carried on feeding the baby as if nothing had happened, going in and out of the birdcage as if it were the most ordinary thing in the world. The story has a happy ending too, because the whole family finally fledged successfully and flew off. But hoopoes are rare breeders in this country, so I am not going to suggest that we all invest in birdcages.

Mute swans often try to nest on tidal sandbanks or below the high-water mark along estuary shores. They seem unable to grasp the fact of tidal movement, and as fast as they build a nest the rising tide washes it away. Locals come to the rescue, constructing swan rafts of empty oil drums or pallets. Anchored suitably and with some vegetation piled on them, the swans will often take over and complete their nest, lay eggs, brood and hatch the cygnets; every time the tide comes in, the nest rises gently and floats, serene and safe.

All over Europe there are traditions that have led people to encourage birds to adopt man-made nest sites. In many villages in Germany, a cartwheel is fixed to the top of a high pole in the hope of attracting a stork to nest. And in Switzerland and Holland they have developed a successful pole-top nestbox for kestrels. If you have a large secluded garden in good kestrel country (and this includes cities), you might consider the experiment of putting up one of these boxes (details in the BTO booklet by Chris du Feu, page 180). Kestrels are among those species which have learned to take advantage of the urban life, taking over window-boxes high up on tower blocks. Nowadays kestrels breed freely in towns, and even peregrines have taken to city life.

Traditionally herring gulls nested colonially on sea cliffs, but they find the rooftops of seaside towns a welcome substitute, especially as they find a ready supply of sandwiches and fastfood leftovers. But they have aggressive habits and not everyone loves them.

Basic types of nestbox

There are two basic types of nestbox: an enclosed space with a small entrance hole, and a tray or ledge with or without sides and roof. The closed type tends to be the most successful, partly because the average house and garden don't offer many convenient cavities reached by a suitable tunnel, and mainly because most of the birds which are prepared to live close to us derive from a woodland habitat.

A variety of nestboxes is readily available from commercial suppliers (see page 180) and, if you want to make your own, there is plenty of information about the science of nestbox materials, construction, fixing, siting and preserving in a definitive booklet by Chris du Feu (see page 180).

However, beware of novelty designs which owe more to sentiment than biological requirement, i.e. boxes whose dimensions are incorrectly formulated or which offer footholds to predators in the shape of ornamental windows and chimneys and, in some cases, unnecessary perches. Rustic boxes, made of hollowed-out birch branches, are perfectly satisfactory, although the wood deteriorates rapidly and they don't last many seasons. But there seems little point in going to all the trouble of making them when they are usually fixed to almost any tree but a birch, thus losing the possible advantage of camouflage. Plain square boxes are the easiest to make, and there is precious little evidence that the birds mind one way or another. The interior size, entrance hole size and the placing of the box are what count most.

Blue tits breed most successfully in an area with plenty of deciduous trees, where there is an abundance of caterpillars.

Siting and fixing nestboxes

Siting the box is a critical affair. The main criteria are protection from the elements and from enemies. First consider the life-style of the intended occupant when you choose a place for it. Tit boxes should be attached to walls or trees, or anything that makes some kind of substitute for a tree, which is where they will be looking for likely entrance holes.

The open plan boxes for blackbirds, robins and spotted flycatchers should be placed against a wall where they are hidden in a dense jungle of ivy or some other creeper, or in a thick hedge, or in a fruit tree where there is some cover, and so on. They are best fixed in discreet crutch sites, invisible to the outside world. The birds will find them.

Ideally the nestboxes should be fixed in position in October or November. This gives them a chance to weather into their surroundings, and their potential occupiers have plenty of time to get used to them and to explore their possibilities. It may well be that they will be used during the winter months as a roost box. However, there are plenty of records of songbirds – and kestrels, too – taking over a nestbox in the breeding season on more or less the day it was erected. Put them up as soon as they are available. Most garden nestboxes should be fixed at about 1.5m to 1.8m (5–6ft) above the ground. Factors such as possible disturbance will obviously affect the decision, and it is worth remembering that birds will nest at heights ranging from ground level to tree top. In order to protect them from hot sun and wet Atlantic winds, the general rule is that the opening should face somewhere in the arc from north through east to south-east, but if it is well sheltered this question of orientation is probably not significant. Nestboxes do not need to be hidden away in a dense clump of trees, or in the middle of a vast woodland. It is better to site them at the edge of a copse, or ride, at the interface between lawn or grass field and the trees. This is the kind of country which gives the best feeding return. There must be an uninterrupted flight path to the entrance, and a distinct lack of places for cats to lie in wait. A convenient staging post some 1.8m (6ft) away may be an asset. This can be anything from a clothes-line to a twig, by way of a specially stuck-in post.

Firm fixing for nestboxes is not a prime requirement, after all, birds often build nests in places which sway with the wind. Even boxes which literally hang from tree branches are successful. But for all that it probably makes good sense to fix securely, and no one, least of all the occupant, wants the box to collapse because of an inadequate screw or rusty nail. And fix the box by way of a batten which will help to ensure that it does not become permanently wet and disintegrates prematurely. Many clutches are drowned in natural nest-sites every year, so take particular care to see that rainwater cannot find its way into the box, remembering that a lot of rain trickles down

Different species have different ideas of what makes the perfect nestbox. From top to bottom: owl, treecreeper and robin boxes.

a wall or tree trunk, and that it tends to follow well-established channels. Make sure the box stands proud of them, or to one side. Incline the box outwards with a slight slant, so that drips from the projecting roof do not go through the entrance hole. Do not worry if the floor of the box, when set up, is not quite horizontal. The birds will solve this problem when they import nest material.

If you want to erect the box against a particular fine tree causing least damage, use trenails as the old-time shipwrights did when nailing planks to frames in 'wooden walls'. These conical pegs of oak or iroko do the job perfectly well and will not damage the tree (or the saw in due course). Alternative choices are to use plastic-covered wire and 'whip' the box to the branch (but this will have to be replaced each season to avoid constricting growth), or to use copper nails which are relatively soft and kind to the forester's saw.

How many boxes?

It is not easy to suggest the number of boxes you should erect for any given species. The quantity depends both on the availability of natural sites and on the local food potential, natural and artificial. But first consider the life-style of your intended occupant. It is a waste of time, for example, to expect two pairs of robins to set up house in close proximity, though it may well make sense to put up more than one box in the hope of getting one occupied. Robins are fiercely territorial, blackbirds slightly less so, but they won't object to other species living close by. So your robin boxes can be close to a tit box. Tits, too are aggressive, status-seeking birds, so don't put tit boxes close to one another.

Other birds, such as house martins and house sparrows remain colonial, enjoying sociability and the safety of numbers.

In a hard winter small birds like wrens look for warmth and an out-of-season nestbox may be just the job for a conglobulation.

Nesting materials

If you provide suitable materials, birds will enthusiastically collect them. In the breeding season, when the scrap and peanut cages are not required for food, they can be packed with straw, feathers, dog or cat combings, short bits of cotton, cotton-wool, sheep wool, etc. In the garden, this may reduce the amount of thieving the sparrows and jackdaws will indulge in when they try to unravel the string from your beanpoles, or tease out threads from your clothes on the washing-line. Tree species will prefer your offerings to be hung from the branches. But put some at ground level, in a mesh bag perhaps, firmly pegged so that they can't be carried away in bulk.

If the weather is particularly dry in May, when the house martins are busy plastering their nestcups, it may be helpful to pour a couple of buckets of water over the earth in a likely place, e.g. along a dusty country lane or over a well-worn bare earth patch on the lawn or in a park. The birds sometimes have difficulty in finding mud puddles from which to pick up their nest gobbets.

The collection of nest material offers an opportunity to the newly engaged pair of birds to reinforce their pair bond, when they offer and exchange particularly choice pieces. In the case of rooks, for instance, you will see them, at the chosen nest site, excitedly passing sticks to and fro with much exaggerated posturing and ritual exchanges of compliments. And, for many species, when the nest is completed the exchanges will continue, the cock bird offering food morsels instead of twigs in the ritual courtship feeding – a procedure that provides the female with nourishment to help form the eggs and keep her alive during the period of incubation. The hens of some species obtain more than a third of their food from their mates during the early part of the feeding season.

Whatever the type of nest, and wherever it is built, whether in nestbox or natural site, its object is the same – to create a cup that will hold the eggs in warmth and yet retain a measure of security from predators and shelter from the elements. It may range from the casual few twigs of a pigeon to the most elaborate nursery of a goldfinch. (In the case of some seabirds and raptors, there may be no nest at all, but in those cases the eggs are well protected by other factors.)

Leave them in peace

If you are lucky enough to be successful in enticing a breeding pair to your nestbox, keep any inspection to a minimum. Be thoughtful with your photography, and in particular be extremely sensitive with any 'gardening' you may be tempted to do with natural nests which don't quite suit your angle of view. You may, inadvertently, betray the nest to a predator. If you are recording the progress of your nests for the BTO's Nest Record Scheme (page 91), keep your visits to a minimum. The well-being and safety of the birds is paramount – put their interests first. If you want to count the young, wait a few days from hatching in the case of small birds. And don't creep up on the nest with exaggerated fairy footfalls. Better to let them know you're coming. It is also important not to disturb nests at the stage when their occupants are close to leaving, since there is a danger they might 'explode' away and become exposed too soon to the attention of the world at large. However, if this disaster should occur, collect the chicks in a handkerchief as best you may and post them back home. Then block up the entrance for ten minutes or so, until they have quietened down.

Reducing nestbox losses

Unhatched eggs, dead or disappearing juveniles, are a distressing possibility. Any number of causes may account for them, apart from the natural loss to predators. A dead parent, inexperienced first-time parents that may have failed in their duty, shortage of food at a critical time – all are possibilities. Double check to see whether rainwater, or cold winds, or the sun's heat, or a cat perch, were responsible. And if you are reasonably certain the fault was not yours, reflect that a natural event of this kind is the normal end for an enormous number of nestlings. It is something which is part of the expected scheme of things, not to be dwelled upon unduly.

Many clutches of eggs and broods of young chicks will be lost to squirrels, weasels, cats, crows, magpies and great spotted woodpeckers. The loss rate is highest in the case of open nests, particularly when it is early on in the season and they are least concealed

House martins once built their nestcups on cliffs but they have happily turned to eaves. They may be encouraged by the provision of a few artificial cups.

Strange nests

Every year the newspapers enjoy a silly bird season where nests are photographed in every conceivable odd position. Blackbirds and pied wagtails have nested in every known make of motor vehicle, including aircraft, and often fledged their young successfully in spite of daily trips to the office and back. Rooks have colonized the vertical ladders on the side of refinery chimneys, seeing them as perfect substitutes for trees in an increasingly treeless landscape. And black guillemots nested on the Yell Ferry in the Shetlands, providing the young with daily trips long before they were scheduled to go to sea.

by growing leaves. But even the most sturdily built nestbox will be subject to attack from the ground and the air. Cats will try to hook the contents out with their paws, or lie in wait, sitting on top of the box. Weasels are common garden predators – they are good climbers and able to squirm through even a 29mm (1⅛in) blue tit hole to fish out the eggs or chicks. Grey squirrels simply reach in for their reward, and if the roof or lid or removable wall-piece is not secure, they will knock it off. They may even gnaw their way in by enlarging the entrance. The only remedy for this is to protect the entrance hole with a nestbox plate (suppliers' address page 180). Tying a bundle of gorse branches around the tree trunk, or even around the box itself, will be a deterrent, especially to cats. However, this remedy will not affect the nest raiding propensities of the great spotted woodpecker, a persistent robber. It too will dislodge a loose lid, or enlarge the entrance by chipping until it is big enough for them to get in. The metal plate may do the trick, but with woodpeckers there is the problem that they simply drill themselves a side entrance with their chisel bills to effect an entry. If they are really troublesome then a woodcrete box is the answer. Given the chance, these woodpeckers will take young house martins and sparrows, as well as tits.

Sparrows and starlings may take boxes over from their rightful owners, or intended owners, by sheer brute force. But this is all part of the rich warp and woof of bird life and, given the current decline of both species, we ought to congratulate them.

Four chicks is average for the swallow and there are three weeks between hatching and fledging. Both parents feed the chicks with insects captured in flight. The male parent has the longest tail streamers.

Maintenance

At the end of the breeding season, in say October (but making sure the occupants really have finished), remove the used nests and give the boxes an anti-bug spray. Do the job with caution, for used bird-nests carry risk of human diseases. The nests and box crevices will be home for feather lice, mites, ticks and flea larvae – creatures that can survive long periods without their host – so you will need to scrape them out carefully, rinse well with boiling water and wait till they are dry before dusting with a squirt of pyrethrum, or brush on an end-of-season coat of Creocote or Cuprinol. Then it will be ready for a winter let, primed with some wood shavings perhaps. Moths may over-winter in them, perhaps even toads, mice or bats. Great and blue tits will certainly use them for winter warmth, roosting in solitary splendour. They often take to rather over-lit, but centrally heated, street lamps for overnight roosts. House martins, which frequently produce three broods of young and whose breeding season will often extend into November, roost in family parties in their nest cavities, which must make for a tight fit.

Give the boxes a spring clean before the breeding season, cleaning out any droppings left by the winter occupants. A squirt of pyrethrum will kill the bugs. Prime with a small quantity of wood shavings or hay to offer a welcoming foundation to house-hunters at courting time. And don't forget to wash your hands after handling nestbox interiors.

BIRDS THAT USE NESTBOXES, LEDGES OR RAFTS

Those marked with an asterisk * are given special legal protection and must not be inspected or approached without a licence.

Blackbird
Blackcap
*Brambling
Bullfinch
*Bunting, Reed
Bunting, Snow
Chaffinch
Chiffchaff
*Chough
Coot
*Crossbill
Dipper
*Diver, Black-throated
*Diver, Red-throated
Dove, Collared
Dove, Rock

Dove, Stock
Duck, Tufted
Dunnock
Eider
*Fieldfare
*Firecrest
Flycatcher, Pied
Flycatcher, Spotted
Fulmar
Gadwall
Goldcrest
*Goldeneye
Goldfinch
Goose, Canada
Goose, Greylag
Grebe, Great Crested

Greenfinch
Guillemot, Black
Gull, Black-headed
Gull, Herring
Hawfinch
Heron, Grey
*Hoopoe
Jackdaw
Jay
Kestrel
*Kingfisher
Linnet
Magpie
Mallard
Mandarin
Martin, House
Martin, Sand
Moorhen

Nuthatch
*Osprey
*Owl, Barn
Owl, Little
Owl, Long-eared
Owl, Tawny
*Peregrine
Pheasant
Pigeon, Wood
Pipit, Meadow
Pipit, Rock
Redpoll
Redstart
*Redstart, Black
Redwing
Robin
Rook
Shelduck

Skylark
Siskin
Sparrowhawk
Sparrow, House
Sparrow, Tree
Starling
Swallow
Swan, Mute
Swift
Tern, Common
*Tern, Little
*Tern, Roseate
Thrush, Mistle
Thrush, Song
Tit, Blue
Tit, Coal
*Tit, Crested

Tit, Great
Tit, Long-tailed
Tit, Marsh
Tit, Willow
Treecreeper
Turnstone
Wagtail, Pied
Waxwing
Wheatear
Woodpecker, Great Spotted
Woodpecker, Green
Woodpecker, Lesser Spotted
Wren
*Wryneck
Yellow-hammer

The Nest Record Scheme

The British Trust for Ornithology runs a Nest Record Scheme, in which the object is to collect information about the breeding behaviour of British birds. If you feel you could collect simple, but precise, information about the birds that nest in your garden, and not necessarily in nestboxes, write to the BTO for information (address page 178). The resulting Nest Record Cards make it possible to record the success, or failure, of known birds' nests. Submitting completed cards to central office adds to the existing body of statistical information on bird-breeding biology – for instance, the timing of each species' breeding season, the number of eggs laid and young reared, and how breeding success is affected by such factors as climate and human activity. Little detailed information of this kind existed before the BTO began the work of compiling data on a large-scale basis in the latter half of the 20th century, but by 2002 a million and a quarter nest records involving 232 species, had been completed. The information has resulted in many useful publications involving analyses of these records.

Other work includes the long-running census on heronries, which aims to count the heron nests at a sample of heronries in the British Isles; wader and wildfowl counts through the winter months; the scheme to map the distribution of every species wintering in the British Isles – the *Atlas of Winter Birds*. All these are organized by the BTO. But most bird societies (obtain addresses from your library) have census work of some kind in hand, so it is worth checking with them.

A ringed reed bunting. In winter the population of these birds is much increased.

Bird ringing

The seasonal movements of birds have always fascinated us, and we have long sought to unravel their mystery. In part, there is an element of sport in the pursuit, an enjoyment of the challenges offered in trapping and marking the birds, but there is a more serious purpose, that of discovering more about birds' life styles and population dynamics, information that can be of great value in assessing the ecological effects of changes in land use.

It was in medieval times, somewhere around the 12th century, that the prior of a Cistercian monastery in Germany reported that a man

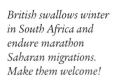

who had fixed a parchment to a swallow's leg asking, 'O swallow, where do you live in winter?' received a reply in the following spring. 'In Asia, in home of Petrus.' The Romans had long used swallows to carry messages to their homes, in the style of pigeon post, but it was in 1740 that Johann Leonard Frisch, a Berliner, attached coloured wool to swallows' legs to discover whether individuals returned to the same nest site year after year. They do!

In the early 19th century, J. F. Dovaston, one of the pioneers of field ornithology, repeated this experiment, fastening cello wire round the swallows' necks. He also attached a copper tag inscribed in Latin, 'Where hast thou gone to from Shropshire?', though sadly he had no returns. The credit for the first use of a bird ring which carried its own unique number, and a return address, goes to a Danish ornithologist, H. C. Mortensen, who ringed 164 starlings in 1899. In Britain, systematic bird ringing began in 1909, sponsored by the publisher H. F. Witherby in London, the founder of the magazine *British Birds*, and A. Landsborough Thompson in Aberdeen. Since 1937 it has been organized by the BTO and only accredited ringers may take part. By 2005, 32 million birds had been individually marked with rings; of these, over 600,000 have been reported back to the BTO.

Trapping, for the purposes of ringing, is based on the methods used by hunters through the centuries, though one of the most ancient techniques, that of liming, is thankfully illegal nowadays. At one time holly bark was stripped in quantities, in the springtime, pounded and mashed by druggists who then supplied the resulting 'birdlime' to hunters. They spread it liberally on suitable roosting-places, where unfortunate songbirds became stuck to their perch. Cage-trapping, decoying, cannon or rocket netting, recordings of bird song – these

British swallows winter in South Africa and endure marathon Saharan migrations. Make them welcome!

are all methods used to bring birds to the hand. The most efficient, at the present time, is the use of mist nets made from fine nylon or terylene thread and dyed black. Erected between tall poles to form an almost invisible barrier, mist nets trap any bird that flies into them. The trapped bird may be marked with a brightly coloured dye, which can be seen from a fair distance. However, this method provides only a limited amount of information and lasts only until the wearer moults to a new flying suit. A bird may also carry a colour ring which is useful in a limited sense in connection with a small number of individual birds in a relatively restricted area.

Far and away the most useful method of marking is the use of numbered metal rings which carry a return address. In Britain the BTO rings are engraved with the legend 'Brit. Museum London SW7'. Other countries sport their own legends, every ring carrying a unique group of letters and numbers. The records are computerized and stored according to an internationally agreed filing standardization, and the coverage is almost worldwide. Both ringing and the photographing of birds is governed by the law as laid down in the Wildlife and Countryside Act, and the primary consideration has always been the well-being of the birds themselves.

Once the bird has been ringed and released, the research department of the BTO must sit and wait for subsequent information. From ringing records, the BTO has deduced that the roads are a major cause of bird accidents. For example, 23 per cent of barn owls meet their end as a result of collision with vehicles. Otherwise predators such as birds of prey, dogs and foxes account for many bird losses, while domestic cats are both a major cause of bird death and a helpful source of ring recoveries!

BTO ringing data show that oystercatchers are doing well overall, increasing mightily in England though less well in Scotland. Sometimes waders like these are colour-dyed when caught – making it easier to track the birds' movement without having to catch them. Eventually the dye wears off.

Many and various are the nuggets of information gathered as a result of long-term bird ringing. We know that some birds live long lives, though the average expectancy is very short indeed, especially in the case of songbirds. But an oystercatcher may live 34 years; a herring gull, 32. The oldest recorded swallow covered nearly 400,000km (250,000 miles) on its migration journeys during its 16 years of life; an Arctic tern, 800,000km (500,000 miles) in its 27 years. In cold weather during the exceptionally hard winter of 1963, searching for new feeding grounds, a redwing covered 3840km (2400 miles) in three days. A swift born and bred in Oxford, was recovered in Madrid three days after it left the nest. We know that small birds increase their weight just before migration. A sedge warbler, which weighs about 10g (0.4oz) normally, will build up to more than 20g (0.7oz) thus carrying enough fat to fuel a non-stop flight of 3200km (2000 miles). It completes this distance in just three days, crossing Europe, the Mediterranean and North Africa, possibly even overflying the Sahara to reach Senegal or Ghana, having slimmed down to half its take-off weight and returned to normal. Ornithologist Dr Chris Perrins trapped blue tits at a well-stocked bird table and found that it was visited by more than a hundred different individuals in the course of the morning, while many of us had assumed that our bird table was feeding just the locals.

The mass of information gives muscle to those seeking to influence legislation in a manner that pays due respect to bird requirements both at home and abroad. Birds themselves recognize no political barriers and need to be conserved on a world-wide basis. After all, our ospreys and avocets are shot in Spain and North Africa; our linnets and redpolls are trapped in Belgium and France. And, at long last, we can map the precise routes of the European swallows when they leave us to winter in the south. Our British swallows, for instance, make their way to South Africa, and I have watched them funnelling in to roost in the reedbeds of a Johannesburg city park, where the local ringers operate their mist nets.

Grey heron populations in Britain have been systematically censused since 1928. The species has had its ups and downs but is currently more abundant than ever, benefiting from reduced persecution and cleaner waterways as well as the feeding opportunities at gravel pits and freshwater fisheries.

Returning bird rings

Over 30 million birds have been ringed to find out about their movements and survival. If you find a ringed bird – dead in the road or brought in by the cat for instance – write to the BTO with the details. These should include the ring number and address, where and when you found it, what had happened to the bird, what species you think it was, and if dead whether it was fresh, old or mummified. Up-to-date avian flu advice is available from the BTO website www.bto.org. Finders are always told about the origins of the bird they report, so include your own address. The only exception is in the case of racing pigeons (their rings are usually encased in plastic and not split), when you should write to the Royal Racing Pigeon Association (address page 179).

BREEDING SEASONS OF BRITISH GARDEN NESTING BIRDS

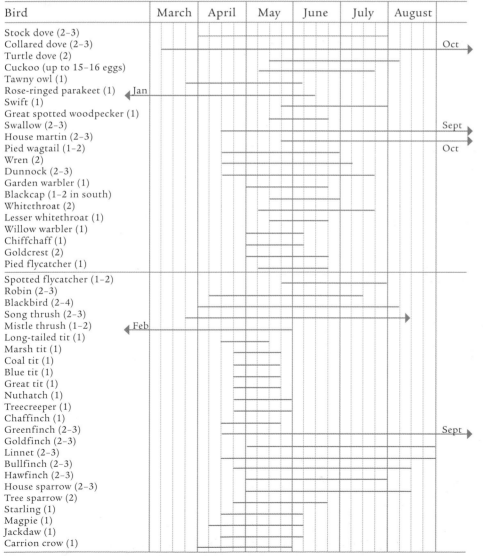

Bird	March	April	May	June	July	August	
Stock dove (2–3)							
Collared dove (2–3)							Oct
Turtle dove (2)							
Cuckoo (up to 15–16 eggs)							
Tawny owl (1)							
Rose-ringed parakeet (1)	Jan						
Swift (1)							
Great spotted woodpecker (1)							
Swallow (2–3)							Sept
House martin (2–3)							
Pied wagtail (1–2)							Oct
Wren (2)							
Dunnock (2–3)							
Garden warbler (1)							
Blackcap (1–2 in south)							
Whitethroat (2)							
Lesser whitethroat (1)							
Willow warbler (1)							
Chiffchaff (1)							
Goldcrest (2)							
Pied flycatcher (1)							
Spotted flycatcher (1–2)							
Robin (2–3)							
Blackbird (2–4)							
Song thrush (2–3)							
Mistle thrush (1–2)	Feb						
Long-tailed tit (1)							
Marsh tit (1)							
Coal tit (1)							
Blue tit (1)							
Great tit (1)							
Nuthatch (1)							
Treecreeper (1)							
Chaffinch (1)							
Greenfinch (2–3)							Sept
Goldfinch (2–3)							
Linnet (2–3)							
Bullfinch (2–3)							
Hawfinch (2–3)							
House sparrow (2–3)							
Tree sparrow (2)							
Starling (1)							
Magpie (1)							
Jackdaw (1)							
Carrion crow (1)							

Breeding season as shown is taken from average dates of first laying (south of England) to approximate fledging of last brood. For seasons in northern England and Scotland start one week to ten days later.

The usual number of broods reared in a season is shown in brackets. There will be many exceptions; for example in good years single-brooded species may suddenly nest twice; some individual pairs of single-brooded species (e.g. blue tit, great tit) may produce two broods in any given season.

Water

All birds need a ready supply of clean fresh water. This chapter looks at some of the best ways we can contribute to this by providing a bird bath or a pond in our own garden, features that, as well as helping birds and other creatures, will give a constant source of amusement and delight to the garden wildlife watcher.

Importance of water supply

A healthy bird gets most of its liquid requirements from its food, but it still requires access to water partly because it will drink a little, but mainly because it bathes a lot. Birds don't sweat: if they get overheated they open their mouths and gape to lose heat. The moisture lost through gaping and through excretion must be replaced. Some species are adapted to a minimal water intake. Desert birds like the budgerigar can go for long periods in the wild without drinking even though they are living on a dry diet of seeds. Tree-living species may sip from foliage after rain, and for this reason there may be some sense in providing a drinking bowl well off the ground. Many town birds visit roof gutters to drink and to bathe.

Drinking

Most birds drink by dipping their bills into the water, then raising their heads to allow the liquid to run down their throats. But pigeons keep their bills in the water, sucking it up and into the system in bulk, a method which is quick and leaves the bird at risk for the shortest time. Swallows, martins and swifts will drink in flight in a shower of rain, or from the surface of the pond, swooping gracefully to dip in momentarily. And, like other birds, they enjoy bathing in rain or even flying through the spray of a lawn sprinkler. However, they will be cautious of bathing in a downpour, since the object of bathing is to wet the plumage but not to soak it to the point it is waterlogged.

Muddy puddles are important to housemartins.
They collect mud in their beaks for nestbuilding.

Bathing

The function of bathing is to maintain the bird's plumage in tip-top condition, mainly because of its importance in flight and thermal insulation. Birds need to bathe even in the depths of winter, since ill-kept plumage will not serve the purpose of keeping warmth in and cold out. Birds, like mammals, are warm-blooded creatures, maintaining a high and constant metabolic rate. Their body temperature is kept up by internally generated heat, as opposed to the system endured by reptiles and fishes whose body temperatures fluctuate in sympathy with that of the ambient environment.

The bathing process, in birds, is highly ritualized. First the plumage is made wet, but not too wet. (Caught in a heavy downpour of rain, birds will hunch and stretch up, so that the water runs off quickly.) Next, the excess drops are shaken off before the oiling stage begins. Twisting its tail to one side, the bird reaches its bill back to collect fatty oil from the preen gland on its rump. The oil is then

After they bathe, preening. Collared doves comb each and every feather.

carefully smeared all over its feathers; the difficult job of oiling the head involves using the feet. After oiling, which is characteristically an urgent process, comes the more leisurely task of preening, the final stage of the ritual, where the bird nibbles and strokes its feathers, one by one, into shape. It then stretches and settles for a period of contemplation.

Pigeons will actually bathe in rain, leaning over with raised wing, presenting themselves to the rain drops. But most birds, like us, seem more concerned to avoid that kind of wetting. Wet plumage means less flying efficiency. When sitting in the open on a nest, birds will hunch themselves in an attitude which sheds rain as quickly as possible, and there is an astonishing record of a moorhen which deliberately covered itself with a handy plastic sheet to keep dry. This was seen by a photographer who was keeping a close watch on the nest (while staying dry in his hide).

Sunbathing

Like many other animals, birds will sunbathe. On
occasion their relaxed posture and gaping beaks
may indicate heat distress, but there's little doubt
that they sunbathe deliberately, probably for a
beneficial chemical effect. The ultraviolet rays of
the sun shining on the feathers produce vitamin D,
subsequently consumed during preening. The warmth of the
sun may also stimulate parasites to expose themselves to capture, or
again birds may simply get pleasure from sunbathing. They certainly
have favourite places for it, like a sheltered doorstep or roof.

*When you first see a bird
laid out gasping in the
sun, you might think it
near deaths door – in
fact it is so relaxed it
is nearly asleep.*

Dust-bathing

Dust-bathing is a speciality of sparrows. The dustbath of fine sand or earth is scuffed up
into the plumage and then shaken and preened off again. It is nothing like as common-
place as water-bathing, and may be another method of dealing with parasites. Unless your
garden is on sandy ground, you may like to provide a dust bath for sparrows and wrens.
The dusting-place should be well sheltered, with some cover nearby, and can consist of a
couple of square feet of well-sifted sand, earth and ash to a depth of a few inches. Sprinkle
the dust bath with bug powder or spray every now and again, for the common good.

Anting

'Anting' is the oddest form of bathing. Birds like starlings and thrushes encourage ants
to squirt formic acid onto their plumage. There are two distinct techniques: one is to
pick up an ant in the bill and hold it against the feathers, urging it to deploy its defence
weaponry by squirting; the other is simply to get in the way of the ants and allow them
to swarm all over the bird's body angrily squirting in protest.

This behaviour is doubtless connected with the process of feather maintenance and
parasite control. There must be some chemical
interaction between ant-acid and the
feathers: formic acid is
insecticidal, so it must
be bad news for feather
mites and bugs. Anting is
directed specially to the ends of
the wing feathers. In preening, these
brush against the head, and a bird's head
is particularly lousy, so perhaps there is a
special incentive to dress it with formic acid.

Sparrows enjoy dust bathing.

Feathers and their function

Feathers are nothing less than an engineering marvel, and they have much to do with the bird success story, precisely designed for their several tasks. They are purpose-built extensions of the skin, horny growths similar in origin to our own fingernails. Light but strong, amongst other things they provide lift surfaces which, powered by all that muscle, enable the bird to fly. Their surface area is large, compared with the weight involved, and their ingenious design allows for continuous maintenance and ruffle-smoothing. And when a part has come to the end of its useful life, after much wear and tear, it may be replaced without withdrawing the aircraft from service.

Designs for flight

The power of flight gives birds the key to world travel. An Arctic tern will spend the summer nesting in high latitudes, then strike south to 'winter' in the Southern Ocean, incredible though that may seem to us. From its point of view it is simply making the best of both worlds. Not all birds use their feathers to propel them across the world. Flight has other values. Instant escape from enemies, airborne invasion of an area rich in caterpillars, or fast approach and capture of prey: all these things are possible with feathers. And different birds have different designs to fit them best for different purposes. A swift has narrow, sweptback wings, designed for speed and aerial fly-chasing; its take-off and landing performance is poor. A pheasant has broad, short wings, giving a powerful near-vertical take-off for instant escape, although it pays for the facility with low endurance, needing to land again within a short distance – far enough away, though, to keep out of trouble.

Jays also bathe in ants, seeming to be in a trance, extending a wing down into the ant nest to encourage the insects to climb up and 'attack' the bird by squirting formic acid, which acts as an insecticide against the feather lice.

Given the power of flight, an animal may more easily escape enemies and take advantage of the benefits of migration to seek fresh food sources and avoid severe weather. Feathers also keep rain from the body, and they insulate a pocket of air against the skin, making it possible to control body temperature. But feathers wear out, and need periodic replacement; moulting provides a new suit of clothes. This shedding and renewal of plumage is timed to suit the lifestyle of each species. A migratory species needs to have its plumage in tiptop condition for long journeys. But most of our garden birds, moulting two or three times a year, tend to lose a few feathers, from both sides at a time, so that although they work at reduced efficiency for a while, they have warmth and flight capability all the time.

Wings are not only used for flying. They may be used as legs, as when a swallow struggles to take a few shaky steps on the ground. On occasion they may be used as advertisement hoardings, their colour-reflecting surfaces being held up and displayed in order to intimidate a rival or impress a partner. The wings are then playing their part in the process of avian communication.

Types and patterns

Feathers, too, have functions beyond providing lift and flight (brightly coloured and patterned, feathers are used at courting time to dazzle potential partners or intimidate rivals; patches in wings and tails may act as flight recognition symbols). Soft down feathers insulate the body and keep it warm; waterproof outer contour feathers repel rain and keep it dry. In some species bristly feathers may help to guide flying insects into the gaping maw and in others feathers may protect the face from the stings of bees and wasps. So feather maintenance is a vital part of a bird's daily life. Much time is devoted to bathing, oiling and preening, keeping the tools of the trade in trim and keeping the bird dry, warm and ready for instant take-off. If feathers are badly damaged, they are replaced as part of normal growth. In the ordinary course of wear and tear they will be replaced as part of a continuous moult: a staggered process because at any given time the bird must not be at the disadvantage of having too many feathers out of action. However, ducks and geese follow a somewhat different plan, moulting all their flight feathers in one fell swoop, lying doggo and flightless for a few weeks after the breeding season while they grow a new suit for the migration flight. At this period they present a sorry appearance, but even this 'eclipse' plumage serves a purpose, camouflaging the birds at the time when they are most vulnerable.

In courtship, rival birds display themselves to best advantage. In the case of the goldcrest, this means raising the normally discreet golden cap into a glorious Mohican.

Odd colours

White, or partially white, birds often appear in gardens. A survey that analysed over three thousand occurrences of albinism showed that the six species most commonly affected were blackbird, house sparrow, starling, swallow, rook and jackdaw. Except in the case of the swallow, the phenomenon affects birds that tend to lead somewhat sedentary and sociable lives. The causes are not easily defined: they may have something to do with a dietary deficiency, perhaps associated with a high intake of 'artificial' food offered at bird tables. Certainly albinism appears to be most often noticed in urban and suburban habitats, where bird table food provides a significant proportion of a blackbird's diet.

Whatever the reason, it is a fact that the blackbird is more prone to albinism, partial or total, than any other species. In the true albino, pigment is completely absent, even the beak, legs and eyes being colourless, but most often the condition is partial, with just a patch of white, or perhaps only one white feather. The extent of the whiteness may vary from season to season, and albino or part-albino young may be produced by normal parents as easily as normal young may be produced by albino parents. An individual may show more white as the years go by. Any feather on the bird may be affected, but the head is particularly prone. One can't help wondering to what extent the white blackbird is at a disadvantage, because it is conspicuous and is therefore more vulnerable to predation. But the suburban habitat, while it may be partly responsible, is at least a relatively protected environment. A case of six of one and half-a-dozen of the other?

A partially albino blackbird is feeding a young mouth.

Whiteness is not the only genetic abnormality suffered by birds. Other 'isms' produce varying intensities of reddishness and yellowishness (erythrism and xanthochroism). In my own garden as I write this we have a gloriously honey-coloured blackbird, an example of leucism, where the normal pigment is pale and diluted. Another common plumage abnormality is melanism, where the bird has too much of the dark pigment eumelanin. These melanistic forms have an exaggerated blackness, most commonly seen in Pheasants.

Whatever its colour, plumage must be maintained. Even in the depths of winter, birds must bathe frequently to keep their insulating and flying suit in full working order. Bedraggled feathers waste body heat and make for inefficient flying, and in winter lost energy is not easily replaced.

Bird baths and their maintenance

Ornamental, free-standing bird baths on pedestals or fashionable 'water features' are often poor value from the birds' point of view, though they might improve the look of a garden – a belief which is well understood by the owners of garden centres! The sides are often too steep and the water too deep: 75mm (3in) should be the maximum depth, and the access should be by way of a gradual non-slip slope. Birds like to wade in cautiously and do not belong to the ostentatious-plunge brigade. If you are committed to a bird bath which has a slippery, or glazed, surface, introduce some sand or gravel to make life easier for the intended users.

Feather maintenance means birds need to bathe frequently, but it is a dangerous and stressful time. The object is to wet the plumage, but not soak it. They must be ready for instant take-off and getaway.

   A long plastic plant tray makes an acceptable bird bath, the sort of thing that tends to be some 110cm (43in) long by 20cm (8in) wide and up to 5cm (2in) deep. An inverted dustbin lid will also serve perfectly well. Either will be eagerly used for drinking and for bathing by grey wagtails, spotted flycatchers, bullfinches, chaffinches – as well as the usual blue tits, blackbirds, sparrows and so on. However, the best material is undoubtedly stone, for instance granite, or concrete.

   If the bird bath contains no oxygenating vegetation, it must be cleaned frequently, or there will be a build-up of algae, which will stink. The water should be changed frequently (daily in hot weather), and must be kept topped up. It is best set up in shade, in the open but within reach of cover and safety.

   In cold weather, the ice-free water you put out will be gratefully used. If the bath is of a breakable material, put a tennis ball in it, so that if the water freezes the ball takes the strain. Do not use glycerine or any anti-freeze, which will damage a bird's plumage. It may make sense to cut a piece of thick polythene sheet to line the bath, so that when it freezes you can flip out the ice easily, in order to refill. In icy weather keep the bird bath ice-free by liberal use of boiling water.

Ponds

The facilities offered by a natural or semi-natural pond
are better by far than those of a bird bath. Indeed,
a pond is almost an essential for any self-respecting
bird garden. Properly stocked with oxygenating
plants and supporting a healthy population of
aquatic insects, snails and crustaceans, it will provide
clean water for drinking and bathing birds as well
as a useful food supply. It is also an endless source
of delight for the naturalist.

*Everybody eats
tadpoles   even your
friendly neighbourhood
blackbird.*

A garden without a pond is sadly deficient; it is the
source of much pleasure. You may be visited by dragonflies;
kingfishers may come to take tadpoles, and the community of life
underwater will fascinate for hours. The water's surface tension
supports pond skaters and water crickets, while mosquito and gnat
larvae hang from it. In the open water there is room for sticklebacks,
newts and plankton creatures, especially if you resist the temptation
to introduce those alien goldfish, which muddy the pond. On the
bottom, enriched with the particles of decaying plant and animal
remains, there will be bugs which can survive in an oxygen-deficient
atmosphere – midge larvae and sludge worms. Best of all are the weedy
margins of the pond, where pond snails and caddis grubs graze the
vegetation, newts and tadpoles forage, water beetles and water boatmen hunt their prey. If you have water lilies, then blackbirds may
turn the leaves over and take the flatworm and snail eggs attached
to the underside.

*If an empress chooses
to lay her eggs in your
pond you know you
have a wildlife wet
patch prizewinner!*

Frogs

Frogs may begin their courtship as early as January, although the season goes through to March, according to the area. They may be a long way from the pond when the sap begins to rise, resting the winter away in a nice muddy hole somewhere, and their cross-country journey may be quite spectacular. Even if there are other ponds about, they'll choose to go to the same one each year, crossing roads and fields on the way if necessary. That's when vast numbers of frogs and toads get killed by motor cars. A warm wet night is the best time to see them. And how do they find their way to the home pond? Probably by its smell, its own unique effluvium, wafted down the wind.

The males are first to get to the breeding pond; they are the croakers. They can even croak underwater, because they make the noise by shuttling air back and forth between lungs and mouth. The females arrive to a warm embrace, which may last nearly 24 hours. And there's a great deal of competition. The unmated males get into a frenzy and clutch at anything in their desire for contact. If they clutch at another male, then there is a warning grunt and a prompt disengagement. If it's an ovulating female the male grips her tightly. With vents close together the couple form a fertile production line – eggs first, followed by a sprinkling of sperm – and soon the pond is full of spawn clouds. Each female may lay as many as a couple of thousand eggs but it's a lucky egg that hatches into a tadpole that metamorphoses into a frog that lives to enjoy your grassy lawn in the summer. Frogs are entirely useful creatures to welcome in the garden, eating snails by the bucketful.

A frog he would a-wooing go
Heigh ho! says Rowley.
Nursery rhyme quoted in 'Melismata'
(1611) Thomas Ravenscroft

Toads

Toads will use your pond for mating and producing their long strings of eggs, but they are more choosy than frogs and slower to colonize new breeding ponds. In the cellar, where it is dank and dark, the common toad likes to make his home base. A stay-at-home and tame creature, it is a pity that he is so unattractive to us. Along with other amphibians and reptiles, he is not popular. Poor toad, he likes to make himself at home in a nest scooped under a stone or in a corner of the cellar all day, then he comes out at dusk, or after a shower. He's an excellent climber; many's the time people have suggested that it is impossible for their toad to escape from the cellar, when the great fat beast clearly hasn't gone short of a meal for years. Toads climb so well you may even find them sitting comfortably in an abandoned bird's nest high off the ground. Long-lived and sedentary, they are slow movers, vulnerable yet protected by poison glands in the skin, which make them distasteful to potential predators. Toads have a well-developed memory for locality, and though they may forage long distances for food, they will return safely afterwards. They will come out in the daytime in a heavy shower but, normally, they feed in the late evening and early at night. They eat almost any living thing they can cram in to their mouths.

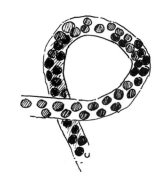

From top to bottom: Toads lay strings of eggs, frogs spawn in clouds and newts lay single eggs, which they wrap in the leaf of a water plant.

Newts

Newts use a different breeding system altogether. The male prepares a parcel of sperm, which he delivers to the female in a courtship ritual during which he swishes his tail to create a current, on which an enticing chemical reaches the female, attracting her up-current to the parcel. She picks it up with the lips of her vent, and the sperms reach the eggs inside. The eggs are fertilized internally.

Try dropping a small piece of raw meat into the pond to find if you have any newts, for they will soon smell it. They will eat almost anything that moves. In midsummer they leave the pond and come ashore for a spell, and at this time will take earthworms and snails. They seem equally happy in the water or out of it.

Pond visitors and predators

Many animals will come to drink and bathe in your pond: birds, grass snakes and slow worms. Hedgehogs will amble over to it and lean in to drink, often enough falling in as well, so it is vital to keep the water-level high and to avoid vertical surfaces, which, if slippery with algae, may defeat even a good climber like a hedgehog. If the pond is big enough, have an island or raft in the centre, providing a safe place for birds to land. Sparrows have been known to land on a lily leaf, and take a quick bath as they slowly sink into the water. Swallows may literally drop in to sip and splash as they fly by. Herons may drop in to sample your fish but also take amphibians and small mammals, with small quantities of reptiles, insects, crustaceans, molluscs, worms and birds. Herons fish mostly at dawn and dusk so they are less often noticed.

Young herons teach themselves to fish, and when they leave their nest in June and July, small garden ponds are attractive to them because they often provide easy fishing. Quite understandably, herons will respond to a garden pond in a comparable way to a blue tit being attracted to a nut feeder.

There is a good reason for increasing the number of garden ponds, since they to some extent replace the gradual decline in the agricultural pond scene. Ponds were once abundant, serving useful purposes for people as well as supporting a large number of aquatic plants and animals. Village ponds provided water for cattle and ducks, and the passing cart in need of a quick wash. The continual coming and going of the animals kept a weed-free area of open water, which was important from the wild animals' point of view, improving the pond's life by diversifying its habitats.

The hunter hunted! This small falcon, a hobby, chases dragonflies to eat them in flight. A summer falcon for a summer insect.

Constructing your own pond

Garden ponds may not have the noble provenance of St James's Park and its wonderful bird-rich lake, but they will give a full measure of pleasure to the owner. It has to be said, however, that there is a certain amount of hard labour involved in the making of even a small one. First of all you must choose the site very carefully; it needs to be level, and must be well away from trees so that it gets plenty of sunlight and does not become clogged with leaves in the autumn.

For a simple pond that will fit even the smallest garden, the equipment and materials required are as follows:

A pond liner, 2.5m × 2m (8ft 3in × 6ft 6in)
Piece of timber, 2m × 75cm × 5cm (6ft 6in × 2ft 6in × 2in)
Ten wooden stakes
Mallet, Spade, Spirit-level
Some sand or old newspaper

The pond liner may be brought from a garden centre, but avoid anything less than 1000 gauge 0.375 microns ($^{15}/_{1000}$in) thick. There are several kinds:

Black polythene cheapest type, but has a limited life of about five years unless protected from sunlight by a covering of earth and stones. Use only water-resistant type.
PVC sheeting more expensive but more resistant to sunlight, best type is strengthened with nylon.
Polyolefin a high grade plastic liner with a life of over fifteen years.
Butyl rubber a very flexible rubber liner with a life of over fifteen years. The best quality liner but the most expensive.

If you choose to line your pond with concrete, the layer should be at least 150mm (6in) thick and must be sealed with bituminous paint or water-seal cement. But be warned that a concrete-lined pond involves back-breaking work. My advice is to plump for a Butyl liner, even though it is expensive.

The smooth newt is the least aquatic of the newts, leaving the pond after the mating season to live on land, hiding under a stone or a log or in the greenery during the day to come out at night to hunt worms and insect larvae.

POND CONSTRUCTION METHOD

1 Mark out the edges of the pond with stakes; if the ground is not level put the shallow end at the bottom of the slope. Hammer in a stake at each end of the pond using the measurements on the diagram on page 109. (It's important to keep to these or the liner will not fit.) Rest the wooden beam across the two stakes and mark a point on the beam 60cm (24in) in from each stake. Find the position of the other stakes by measuring out from these points.

2 You can now start to dig the pond. Put any turves to one side, as you can use them later to fringe the pond. Save the topsoil as well, because this will be put back in the finished pond. The best of the soil could be used to make a bank. Put soil to one side, out of the way of the spread lining.

3 As soon as the hole begins to grow, check that the sides of the pond are at the same level by laying the wooden beam over the pond and checking with the spirit level. Take out the stakes and remove the earth from the higher sides.

4 Use the diagram to work out the different depths of the pond. The deepest part of the pond is a third of the way from the end, and the sides of the pond should shelve up gradually from this point to the edge. Do not make the slope too steep. Check the depths are right by measuring down from the wooden beam. If you dig too deep don't worry – you can always put some soil back!

5 A special feature of the pond is the marshy area at the shallow end. Extend it by removing earth to a depth of 5cm (2in) for a distance of 20cm (8in) from that end.

6 When the hole is ready, pick out any stones or sticks, which may puncture the lining, and pour in some damp sand to make a layer 2cm (¾in) deep over the whole of the pond. This is to give a soft base for the lining to rest on. You could use sheets of spread-out newspaper, but make sure you build up a good layer.

7 Take the liner and with it overlap the deep end of the pond by 20cm (8in). Anchor it with heavy stones, temporarily.

8 Spread out the liner over the pond, and push it gently down into the hole. Don't try to make it fit too snugly as the weight of the water will do that.

9 Fill the pond almost to the top with water (use rainwater if possible – tap water often contains high levels of nitrates). You can now see whether you've made any mistakes in levelling the pond. Any errors can be put right by removing or adding earth under the liner. Make sure that there are going to be water levels of from 2cm to 10cm (¾–4in) at the shallow end.

10 You should wait two or three days to allow the liner to settle, then carefully trim off the surplus plastic round the edge leaving at least 20cm (8in) overlap, but do not cut any off the shallow end. Do not trim too soon, the weight of water drags in a lot of slack. And do not trim too close, or you will have difficulties when arranging your pond surround of stones or turf.

11 Secure the edges of the plastic by burying it under earth or large stones. You can also use the turf for this purpose. If you are using a polythene liner, it's very important to ensure the sheet is totally buried, as in time sunlight will destroy it.

12 Take the topsoil you have saved and sprinkle it over the surface of the pond until you have built up a layer of silt several inches deep over the liner. The earth will form a marshy area at the shallow end. This earth should not be in contact with the surrounding ground or in dry weather water will be drawn out of the pond.

13 Take a couple of large stones, and carefully place them in the shallow end so that they show above the surface. Birds will use these as perching places.

Pond plants

The pond must be properly stocked with suitable plants for it to establish a healthy home for a living community. The plants release oxygen into the water and absorb the carbon dioxide produced by the water animals which are bound to colonize it. Plants also provide food, shade and shelter for the animals. They thrive on plenty of light, but welcome protection from strong winds. There are three main plant categories, free-floaters, oxygenators and marginals. Any aquatic nurseryman can supply them, with planting instructions.

The pond in profile

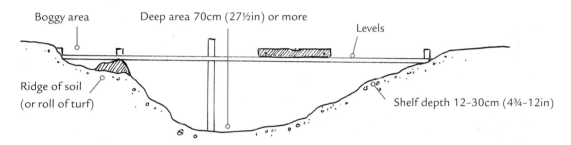

Boggy area
Deep area 70cm (27½in) or more
Levels
Ridge of soil (or roll of turf)
Shelf depth 12–30cm (4¾–12in)

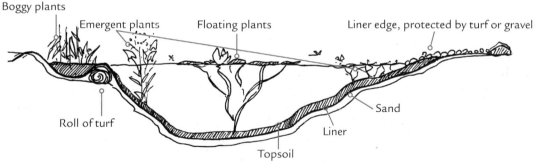

Boggy plants
Emergent plants
Floating plants
Liner edge, protected by turf or gravel
Roll of turf
Sand
Liner
Topsoil

Ideal pond dimensions

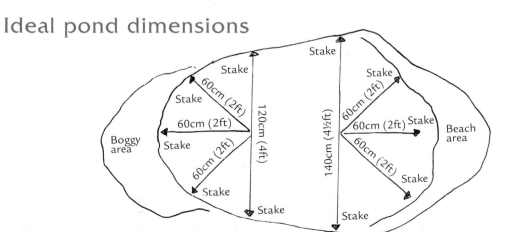

Stake
Stake
Stake
Stake
Stake
Stake
60cm (2ft)
60cm (2ft)
60cm (2ft)
60cm (2ft)
60cm (2ft)
60cm (2ft)
120cm (4ft)
140cm (4½ft)
Boggy area
Stake
Stake
Beach area
Stake
Stake
Stake

Introducing pond animals

Animals will find their own way to your pond, but it makes sense to introduce some common water snails straight away, for they will serve a useful purpose in grazing the algae. Buy them from your aquarist, and remember that cheap ones eat just as efficiently as expensive ones. Ramshorn snails *Planorbis corneus*, or the freshwater winkle *Paludina vivipara*, are the species least likely to attack your 'best' plants. One snail to every 5sq cm (2sq in) of surface water is said to be the desired population, but don't put too many in, they will soon find their own balance.

You may wish to introduce frogs (by way of spawn clouds), toads (spawn strings), water spiders and beetles to suit your own whim. But go easy on the great diving beetle *Dytiscus marginalis*, if you are going to have largish fish, because it will attack them. And avoid newts in a small pond for they will eat almost anything. Most insect species will find their own way – for instance dragonflies, water boatmen and pond skaters. Sticklebacks and minnows will control the mosquito and gnat larvae that will inevitably appear. Again, a rough rule of thumb is 25mm (1in) of fish to 50sq cm (24sq in) of surface area. On the whole it is probably best not to have any fish; they stir up the bottom and will eat your dragonfly larvae.

Birds will enjoy hunting the pond life; you will enjoy the drama. Robins and blackbirds go for tadpoles, blackbirds try for newts, kingfishers enjoy sticklebacks, and if you introduce goldfish or carp, then you may be fortunate enough to be visited by a heron. But goldfish are a mixed blessing; they may look colourful but they are bottom feeders, creating in the process a continuous cloud of mud which means the water is rarely completely clear.

Theoretically, the pond should need little maintenance. When it is first filled and planted it will probably be opaque and green-looking for a while, but as the plants grow the water will clear. In hot weather you may have to add water, especially if you are losing it by capillary action. Devise some way of trickle-feeding it, or diverting rain to it, to save trouble. If it is near trees, then fallen leaves may need to be removed in the autumn, but it should not be necessary to clean the pond out. With well-balanced populations a pond will stay healthy for years.

In the breeding season, house sparrows relish emergent dragonflies.

You will find that the finished product will give you as much pleasure as it does the birds, and if, one day, a heron comes and eats your fish you must grin and bear it and re-stock the pond.

It really isn't possible, or natural, to try to run a sort of 'paradise garden' in which predators have no place. However hard it may be for us to reconcile ourselves to it, the fact is that predators like foxes, sparrowhawks and herons, which prey on and eat other species, are operating in the best interests of the species on which they prey. By catching the slower individuals which are off-colour or sick, they are continually weeding out the less healthy members of a species so that it is the fittest which survive.

Larger ponds

A pond that you can jump across with ease can provide a great deal of enjoyment as well as serving a useful purpose for the birds. But there's no doubt that the possibilities deriving from a larger water area become more interesting. If you live within reasonable proximity to a wildfowl flightline, by a river valley or water course for example, there is every chance that you will attract breeding or wintering ducks. Even a small pool has attracted flighting ducks, but the larger the better. And if your own home patch offers no chances, then why not cast an influential eye on land owned by public corporations or commercial interests? Over the last half-century the great potential of gravel pits in south-east England has been realized, very much to the benefit of water birds and migratory wildfowl.

Large pond construction is dealt with in some detail in a booklet published by the Game Conservancy Trust (address page 179).

An ample and reliable supply of water and food, plenty of shelter for roosting and nest sites: these are the features that make your garden irresistible to a host of birds and other wildlife – the following chapters give you an indication of what you can expect to see, what will try to remain invisible, and some of the less usual visitors.

Moorhens have a well-deserved reputation for kicking and mayhem, but this pair seem to be indulging in a bout of hormonal togetherness, in front of the children.

Species Notes

These notes give basic information about some of those species that patronize feeding stations and artificially provided nest places. They summarize status and distribution, habitat, food and feeding, nest and nesting. There is little information on identification as I am assuming that a field guide is essential to any bird gardener's library.

GREY HERON *Ardea cinerea*

- Resident throughout British Isles, wherever there is water not too deep for wading. Feeds mainly on fish, but much else. Fish farmers objecting to heron visitors should contact the RSPB (for address see page 178). May come to bird table for kitchen scraps; will come to garden pond for goldfish, frogs, etc. Nests in tree canopies, colonially. Single nests sometimes found which may signal the founding of a new colony. Bulky structure of branches, sticks, lined with smaller twigs.
- Artificial nest site: May take advantage of a platform on chicken wire frame firmly placed high in Scots pine or other suitable tree.
- Eggs: 3–5 greenish-blue. February or March. Incubation about 25 days; fledging about 50–55 days. Sometimes two broods.

MUTE SWAN *Cygnus olor*

- Generally distributed. Open water, ponds, parks, sheltered estuaries, sea coast and lochs.
- Dips head and neck, or 'up-ends' to graze on underwater vegetation; also takes roots and buds of aquatic plants, small frogs, tadpoles, fish. Will come to hand or feeding station for bread.
- Nests anywhere near water, on large heap of vegetation.
- Artificial nest site: Takes readily to a suitable raft, both on fresh water and on estuaries provided there is a gentle slope with easy access. Prime with a pile of vegetation.
- Clutch: 5–7 almost white eggs, tinged with greyish- or bluish-green. April or May. Incubation about 35 days; fledging about 4 months. One brood. Warning: aggressive at nest.

CANADA GOOSE *Branta canadensis*

- Introduced to Britain as a status symbol in the 18th century, ornamenting stately lakes. Has since become a very successful feral species, enjoying grassland and marshes by freshwater ponds and lakes.
- Grazes in flocks on grassland. Also takes water plants. Will come to hand-feed on corn or bread when tame.
- Nests on islands and marshes, sheltered by undergrowth or bush. Nest-hollow lined with grasses, leaves, reeds, down and feathers.
- Artificial nest site: Box or platform raised on posts above water level or on raft. Make an artificial island, plant clumps of iris, reeds, sedge, etc. to provide a nest site. Wooden platforms, up to 20m (65ft) above ground, or on top of 3m (10ft) poles where there are no trees, are soon colonized. Try sawn-off barrels or open tubs, suitably drained, and offering a platform some 60cm (24in) across and 30cm (12in) deep.
- Clutch: 5–6 white eggs. Late March or April. Incubation 4 weeks; fledging 6 weeks. One brood.
- Warning: Canada geese (gander especially) can be very aggressive in the breeding season, and have been known to attack people, even wounding children.

MANDARIN *Aix galericulata*

- An exotic dabbling duck which has escaped from waterfowl collections to flourish mainly in the home counties, but increasingly elsewhere.
- Surface and up-ending feeders on vegetation, but mainly graze ashore. Will come to corn on lawn. If wood pigeons make their lives impossible, try offering it in the pond.
- Nests in tree holes, mostly oak and ash, usually 1.5–7m (5–24ft) above ground. Reluctant to take to boxes at first, needs secluded pond or stream with trees nearby.
- Nestbox: Upright box, 50cm (20in) high, 20–25cm (8–10in) wide and deep with a 10cm (4in) entrance hole (any shape). Line with shavings or rotting wood loose enough for bird to hide eggs. Fix at 4.5m (15ft) height, but can be lowered in subsequent seasons if successful.
- Clutch: 9–12 eggs in March, hatch in May, one brood.

The female mandarin duck lines her tree-hole with down to cradle the eggs. The chicks leap out of the hole soon after hatching. Mandarins were introduced from East Asia in the 1930s and have flourished in the southern half of England.

MALLARD *Anas platyrhynchos*

- Generally distributed, near all kinds of freshwater, estuaries and coastal islands.
- Food: Mainly vegetable. Enjoys soft potatoes.
- Nests in thick undergrowth sometimes far from water. Pollard willows, tree holes, secondhand crow nests, etc. Grass, leaves, rushes, feathers.
- Nestbox: Try providing an apple-box or large, open cat basket in typical nesting area. Where mallards have become very tame (village ponds and the like), try erecting an open-ended barrel on an island. Otherwise a mere hollow in the ground, bordered by a couple of short logs and sheltered under a wigwam of spruce boughs, may do the trick. Mallard nests are probably best sited on rafts or islands, where they enjoy some protection from foxes and rats.
- Alternative nestbox: Using sawmill offcuts, make a box with inside dimensions of 30cm (12in) square and 23cm (9in) high. Prime with 25–50mm (1–2in) of woodshavings. Make a tunnel about 30cm (12in) long leading to an entrance hole 15cm (6in) square. This tunnel entrance serves to deter crows. A ramp should lead gently down from the tunnel entrance to the ground. Ease of access is important, not only for the comfort of the duck, but because she might take broods back to the safety of the box at night for the first couple of weeks after leaving the nest, especially in cold weather. The duck likes to be able to see out from the nestbox so provide a horizontal slit in the side.
- Clutch: About 12 greyish-green or greenish-buff, occasionally a clear pale blue. February onwards. Incubation 4 weeks; fledging 7 weeks. One or two broods.

BUZZARD *Buteo buteo*

- Resident and mainly sedentary, widely distributed, having recovered after myxomatosis reduced rabbit populations in the 1950s. Commonest bird of prey over much of Britain. Soaring spiralling flight on broad rounded wings.
- Agricultural country or moorland with plenty of trees. Also mountains and wild coast.
- Pounces on rabbits, small mammals, takes some carrion. Increasingly scavenging bird gardens.
- Bulky nest in trees or cliff ledge. Lays 2–4 blotched red/brown eggs in April or early May, incubated mainly by female 34–38 days. Fledging 6–7 weeks. Single brood.

SPARROWHAWK *Accipiter nisus*

■ Resident and sedentary. Long tail and broad wings. Male has dark slate-grey upperparts and rufous barred underparts; female is larger, with browner plumage. Sparrowhawks fly fast, weaving along hedges, borders and watersides. Well-wooded country, not averse to well-treed gardens, where they may lurk out of sight keeping an eye on the bird table. Hunt by surprise, shock and awe, taking small birds or mammals to a regular plucking post. Female raids bird garden and bird table to take collared doves, blackbirds and starlings; the smaller male takes mostly finches and tits.

■ Nests in trees, often conifers, early May. Untidy mass of sticks lined with fresh greenery.

■ Clutch: 5–6 whitish, blue or reddish eggs, incubated by the female for 32–35 days. Male brings food for female to feed young. Fledging about 4 weeks. Single brood.

Sparrowhawks slip into your garden on silent wings in search of a tasty morsel. This female missed her kill and is posing with the hosta on a flowerpot. Be philosophical, they have to make a living!

RED KITE *Milvus milvus*

■ Once a common scavenger in the streets of Elizabethan England, it was shot, poisoned and collected almost to extinction in the British Isles. Re-introduced to England and Scotland in 1989, scattered populations – most particularly in the East Midlands – may be on the verge of recolonizing the whole of lowland Britain to become a common scavenger again. One of the outstanding breeding successes of recent times, now beginning to visit bird gardens for scraps. If you live in kite country, pieces of chicken or dead day-old chicks may bring them swooping on your lawn, but don't leave them out for the rats when it gets dark.

■ Oakwoods, wooded valleys and hill country. Soars like a buzzard, but with longer and more angled wings, deeply forked tail. An opportunist feeder, taking much carrion.

Red kites are rapidly colonizing Britain after near-extinction. Already there are some 500 breeding pairs – the prediction is that there could be thousands within a decade. These are gathering over a feeding station.

■ Nest is of sticks and mud, alongside the trunk of tall oaks, especially if ivy-covered, often on top of a buzzard or raven nest.

■ Clutch: 1–3 white eggs in early April. Incubation by female for 31–32 days, fledging at 7 weeks or more. One brood.

PEREGRINE *Falco peregrinus*

- Resident and abundant. Now re-established after the population collapsed in the 1960s, and found from Orkney to Dorset on the western half of mainland Britain (and pioneering to the east). Also along the north-east coast of Northern Ireland.
- Pigeons and seabirds such as puffins or kittiwakes are taken on the wing. Some small mammals, including rabbits.
- The nest is a bare scrape, no material, though there may be a scatter of racing pigeon rings, on the ledges of steep cliffs, conveniently close to its preferred prey, pigeons. Logically taking to windowsills or high-rise church ledges in cities where, again, pigeons are plentiful.
- Long record of nesting on man-made structures, for instance in the 1800s on Dunstanburgh Castle in Northumberland. Nest site needs good vantage lookout and roosting perch. Pylons, chimneys, radio towers, power stations, churches and cathedrals.
- Clutch: 3–4 eggs laid on a bare unlined scrape in April. Incubation 28–29 days, fledging in 5 or 6 weeks. Single brood.

KESTREL *Falco tinnunculus*

- Resident, generally distributed, except in winter in far north.
- Moors, coast, farmland and open woodland, suburbs and cities.
- Perches on trees, posts, wires or buildings, watching out for its prey. Hunts in the open, checking frequently to hover in characteristic attitude, watching for beetles or small mammals. Untypically, has been known to come to bird tables to pick at turkey carcasses and day-old chicks, even broken dog biscuit.
- Makes no nest, but uses a scrape on cliff or quarry ledge or uses secondhand crow nest as platform. Sometimes in tree hollow or ledge on building or ruin.
- Nestbox: Open-fronted 63 × 38 × 38cm (25 × 15 × 15in) high, with roof overhanging 5cm (2in). One of the long sides partly open, having only a 12.5cm (5in) board along the bottom part, fitted with a broom pole lip to enable the bird to perch easily before entering. Prime the box with a little peat mould or woodshavings. Fix very firmly on 6–10m (18–30ft)

The buzzard (top) and sparrowhawk (bottom) are fond of soaring, whereas the kestrel (right) typically hunts by hovering then dropping on its prey.

pole, or high on side of house where some shelter is available from midday sun. If fixed to tree, make sure chick thieves cannot climb to it easily, and place it so that wing-exercising juveniles can step out on to a branch (or extend the broom pole sideways). Swiss-erected boxes were positioned near farm buildings, and in one year no fewer than 26 out of 36 were occupied in an area of about 2000ha (5000 acres). With the continuing loss of hedgerow hollow-tree sites it is much to be hoped that these boxes will become more popular with farmers. But a box makes a conspicuous nest site, and unfortunately young kestrels have a ready, though illegal market, so be very careful that they are well protected. Farm buildings, private parkland, nature reserves and sewage farms are ideal sites. In Holland, where farmers encourage kestrels in controlling voles and shrews, the boxes have been highly successful. Little owl, jackdaw, collared dove, stock dove or blackbird may also use them.

- Clutch: About 5 eggs, the white colour often hidden by red-brown splotchings. Mid-April onwards. Incubation 28 days; fledging 28 days. One brood.

PHEASANT *Phasianus colchicus*

- Resident and generally distributed except in Ireland. Much-managed as a game bird. Woodland edge, cultivated land, parkland, large secluded gardens and shrubberies, damp, rushy and sedgy fields.
- Forages on ground for varied selection of animal and vegetable food. Fruit, seeds, grain, insects, worms, slugs. Will come to secluded garden ground station for corn.

First introduced to Britain in the 11th century, pheasants support an important rural industry. There may be nearly two million breeding pairs.

- Nests under cover of ferns, brambles, etc., in woods, copses, hedgerows and reedbeds, making a hollow in the ground and lining it with a few stems of grass and dead leaves.
  - Clutch: 8–15 olive-brown eggs. Early April onwards. Incubation 22–27 days; fledging 12–14 days. One brood.

MOORHEN *Gallinula chloropus*

- Generally distributed, scarcer in northern Scotland. Almost any fresh water from a ditch to a lake; freshwater ponds, slow streams, marshes and watermeadows. Forages on grassland and waterside vegetation. Food is mostly vegetable, but includes a fair proportion of animals, such as worms, slugs and snails. Will soon get used to coming for scraps on the ground; flies less readily up on to the bird table.
- Nests typically in shallow, still water. Platform of dead plants amongst aquatic vegetation, in trees and bushes.
- Nestbox: Will happily take over a duck box, or a mini-island.
- Clutch: 5–11 whitish-grey to buff or greenish eggs. April onwards. Incubation 19–22 days; fledging 6–7 weeks. Usually two broods, frequently three.

HERRING GULL *Larus argentatus*

- Resident, generally distributed along coasts, estuaries, waters and fields often far inland.
- Opportunist feeder, eating almost anything, but mostly animal food. Will come to bird table or ground station but is shy and not particularly welcomed by other birds.
- Nests in colonies on cliff ledges, grassy coastal slopes, sand dunes and shingle. Large nest of grass or seaweed. Of recent years it has taken to nesting on roofs and chimney pot areas where scraps are freely available. Not to be encouraged, though, as it will be aggressive in defence of its young.
- Clutch: 3–4 eggs, olive to umber, sometimes pale blue or green, splotched with deep blackish-brown. End April to early June. Incubation 26 days; fledging 6 weeks. One brood.

Talk gull

The herring gull's mode of communication has been studied for decades. A trumpeting long call is its intent to stand fast. To threaten, it draws itself up to look bigger, lowers the tip of its bill ready to strike, and pulls its 'wrists' out of its bodyfeathers. It then steps towards its opponent stiffly.

BLACK-HEADED GULL *Larus ridibundus*

- Resident, but joined in winter by a large influx of immigrants from the Netherlands and points east. After near-extinction in the 19th century now flourishing and a familiar year-round garden visitor to large urban areas. Most common in winter. Opportunist feeder, scavenging a wide variety of kitchen scraps and more genteel offerings. Summer visitors to the garden will be mostly juveniles (brown wing feathers). In winter plumage the adults lack the conspicuous chocolate brown cap.
- Clutch: 2–3, incubation 22–24 days, fledging about 5 weeks. Single brood.

Kittiwakes find sympathetic nest ledges on warehouses and rooftops, an acceptable substitute for their cliffside colonial gatherings.

KITTIWAKE *Rissa tridactyla*

■ Nests in colonies on precipitous sea-cliff ledges. Enjoys man's hospitality by colonizing cliff-ledge-like warehouse window-ledges. Also inside motor-car tyres hung as dockside fenders. Needs shoe-box size ledge on vertical surface overhanging water, when it builds a neatly constructed nest of grasses, seaweed and so on, often cantilevered out over the abyss.

■ Clutch: 2 eggs, pale blue/brown, at the end of May or early June, incubated by both sexes for 26–28 days. Fledging about 6 weeks. Single brood.

FERAL PIGEON *Columba livia*

■ Resident and generally distributed. Derived from the ancestral rock dove by way of dovecotes, now a common bird of towns and cities throughout much of the world. A fearless visitor to bird gardens, often joined by racing pigeons which are either 'resting' or have opted out of the race.

■ Rock doves were distinguished by a pale back with a white rump and two distinct black wingbars, but this domesticated version offers a variety of plumages.

■ Food is chiefly grain, seeds of all kinds. Will take sandwich left-overs, but much prefers a piece of cheese.

■ Nests on roofs, ledges on buildings, bridges and so on; less at home on trees, evidence of their ancestral home on the ledges of sea cliffs. Nest is just a few scraps of locally sourced material, a meagre cup holding two white eggs. Incubation 16–19 days by both sexes, fledging 35–37 days, at which point the parents may already be sitting on the next clutch. The young may breed at 7 months. No wonder they are symbols of fertility! Multi-brooded (3–5) throughout the year, by virtue of feeding the squabs for the first few days on the 'milk' they secrete from the lining of the crop. In this way they avoid the necessity of hatching chicks at a time when, for instance, caterpillars are abundant, the requirement which encourages most small birds to produce young in late spring.

Wood pigeon display is active and noisy – they clap their wings and indulge in spectacular climbing, clapping and diving flights. But here the amorous cock in the middle is about to be thumped by a rival on the left.

WOOD PIGEON *Columba palumbus*

- Resident and generally distributed except in extreme north of Scotland. Open country of all kinds, provided there are some trees.
  - Feeds mainly on ground, but in spring will graze over foliage, buds and flowers in trees. Main food vegetable: cereals, roots, beans, peas and seeds. Will come to garden feeding station for ground food, bread, vegetable scraps, seeds, and may even visit the bird table. Partial to beans and peas, an often unwelcome visitor on account of its healthy appetite.
- Nests in tall hedgerows, almost any kind of tree, secondhand crow nests and squirrel dreys. Sometimes on ground or on building ledges in towns, where it has overcome shyness. Few twigs (you can often see the outline of the eggs if you stand under the flimsy nest).
- Clutch: Normally 2 white eggs. April to September, though they have been found in every month of the year. Incubation 17 days; fledging about 3 weeks. Two or three broods usually.

Collared doves are less extravagant than wood pigeons in display, they glide in sensuous love-making, when the male may give a gentle nudge of encouragement. Now one of the commonest birds in Britain having first arrived to breed in the mid 1950s after a long drawn-out migration from India.

COLLARED DOVE *Streptopelia decaocto*

- Resident and widely distributed. Vicinity of farm-buildings, park-like places and gardens in towns and villages. In the early 1950s this species did not figure on the British List, yet it is now found throughout the country, the result of a remarkable cross-Europe invasion originating from India.
  - Finds its food in close relationship with humans, sharing grain and chickens, raiding corn and stackyards. In parks and gardens will also take berries and young foliage. Comes freely to a bird table and ground feeding station for seeds, peas, grain and scraps.
- Nests in trees, preferably conifers, on a platform of sticks, grasses and roots.
- Clutch: 2 white eggs. February to October. Fledging 21 days. Several broods.

TAWNY OWL *Strix aluco*

- Resident and generally distributed in Britain, but never recorded wild in Ireland. Woodland, farmland, parks and well timbered gardens.
- Hunts at dusk for small mammals, birds and insects, even frogs and newts. May take bats such as noctules or pipistrelles. May take scraps – and small birds – from bird table.
- Nests in tree holes, secondhand crow, hawk and heron nests, squirrel dreys. Sometimes in barns and on rocky ledges. Branch may need sawing above hole to prevent loss of nest site owing to gales. Listen on a quiet night in January to map their territories and find a likely spot for a box.
- Nestbox: Enclosed with 20cm (8in) diameter hole at top, inside depth 76cm (30in), floor 20 × 20cm (8 × 8in). Will use a barrel: 180 litre (40 gallon) is best, but 27 litre (6 gallon) has been used successfully. If a hole is opened in it and the barrel fixed to a tree crutch about 3.5–9m (12–30ft) high, although the height is probably not critical. Or might use a barn owl box.
- The chimney type nestbox has four wooden planks at least 76cm (30in) long and 20cm (8in) wide butted on to each other, using 5cm (2in) oval nails, to make a square-sectioned chimney. A 23 × 23cm (9 × 9in) base, which must be perforated by at least half-a-dozen drainage holes, is nailed to one end to form the floor. A thin sheet of ferrous metal is to be preferred to either perforated zinc or a wooden floor. A layer of dry peat or sawdust should be added to the completed base to counteract the fouling that will occur in the fledging period. Chimney boxes of this size are too deep for a hand to reach to the bottom, either for examining, ringing the nestlings, or for cleaning out. Make an observation door on one side of the box 20 × 15cm (8 × 6in), hinged to the back of the box and fastened at the front by a hook-and-eye catch. Fit the box under a lateral tree bough at an angle of about 30° from the vertical. If attaching to main trunk contrive an angle of about 45° to simulate a broken branch. Secure to the tree by wire bands at both top and bottom, but remember these will rust through, or become embedded in bark, so watch your maintenance. These boxes have also been used by kestrels, robins, great tits, jackdaws and starlings. In Scotland, a box might attract a pine marten. Be cautious, tawnies can be dangerous.
- Clutch: 2–4 white eggs. February to early April. Incubation 28–30 days; fledging about 4 weeks. Owlets are adventurous, clambering about branches when they sometimes fall, but are amazingly able to climb back using strong claws. One brood.

SWIFT *Apus apus*

- Summer resident, generally distributed except in north-west Scotland. Late to arrive – end April, early May; first to depart – early August. Habitat exclusively aerial. Rarely on ground except at nest. Feeds on the wing, taking only insects, anywhere from ground level to 300m (975ft).
- Nests in colonies, under eaves, in crevices and in holes. Bits of straw, grass, feathers, seed fluff, collected on the wing and stuck together with saliva to form a cup.
- Nestbox: Using a plank 1.65m × 20cm × 10cm (65 × 8 × ¾in), make a box 50 × 20 × 14cm (19½ × 8 × 5½in) with an entrance hole cut in the floor of the box (not the end, as swifts prefer to enter vertically from below). Make box longer than 50cm (19½in) if convenient, but not shorter, as they like to nest at least 30cm (12in) from the entrance hole. Prime nest area with a ring of twisted straw. Cut an inspection door 15 × 20cm (6 × 8in) at rear roof to aid cleaning (or buy the commercial version). Site it under the eaves at least 3.5m (12ft) above ground, up to 30m (100ft) if necessary. Block entrance hole till swifts first arrive, at the end of April or the beginning of May, in order to discourage earlier nesting sparrows and starlings. Sensitive to disturbance. In spring, when incoming swifts first arrive, play a CD of swift calls (available from Jacobi Jayne, see page 180) in the hope of attracting them to your nestboxes.
- Alternative plan: Open out a narrow slit in eaves to allow entrance to your roof.
- Clutch: 2–3 white eggs. Late May, early June. Incubation 18–19 days; fledging about 6 weeks. One brood.

Brightly coloured plant and bird! Yellow flag and kingfisher.

KINGFISHER *Alcedo atthis*

- Resident and generally distributed, except in Scotland, having benefited from the improved water quality of once-polluted waterways. Streams, rivers, canals, lakes, estuaries (especially in winter). Perches or hovers above water, fish-watching. Plunges to capture small fish, insects, larvae and amphibians. In winter, visits coast for shrimps, prawns, small rock-pool fish, etc. May come to garden ponds for minnows or sticklebacks. Nests in tunnels in banks of streams or sand pits, boring 5cm (2in) tunnels as far as 1.2m (4ft) to a nest chamber, preferably in sandy soil.

■ Artificial nest-site: Bore a 15° upward sloping tunnel into an uncluttered vertical or near-vertical north-east facing stream bank. At least 1m (39in) of bare face is needed to discourage predators. The tunnel should be 10cm (4in) wide and 6cm (2½in) high and at least 90cm (3ft) or so above high-water mark. Leave birds to excavate nest-chamber or use ingenuity to create a chamber 17.5cm (7in) round and 12.5cm (5in) high. Or, will excavate tunnel if an artificial bank is provided beside a suitable stream. Fix fencing posts, e.g. willow, which may sprout even if embedded in concrete. Stretch 63mm (2½in) mesh chicken wire or square mesh pig wire, to a height of 1.2m (4ft) or more to make a vertical face, facing north if possible, with a degree of privacy and foliage. Fill in behind wire wall with sand or sandy soil. Provide perches and posts nearby. There is no need to cut entrance hole in the netting. The Wildfowl Trust at Arundel in Sussex had success with this design.

■ Clutch: 6–7 white eggs. Late March to September. Incubation 19–21 days; fledging 23–27 days. Two, maybe three broods.

RING-NECKED PARAKEET *Psittacula krameri*

■ This African/Indian species has been colonizing the Home Counties and the Thames Valley since first escaping from captivity (or being deliberately released) in the late 1960s, first reported breeding in 1969.

■ Omnivorous, relying heavily on bird tables. Enjoys fruit and garden opportunities. Offer dates, if you can afford them. Tiresome habit of pecking at apples before sampling the next one. Potential orchard pest.

Watch out for this one. Is the monk parakeet going to be next to colonize? Small populations have tried to establish in the past; currently there is a small presence of breeding birds in Hertfordshire.

■ Flocks now breeding successfully and spreading. Suburban parks, large gardens. Nests in tree holes, when it may take over a woodpecker cavity. Presumably it will take to enclosed boxes placed high up in a tree.

■ Clutch: 3–4 white eggs from January to June, incubation 22–24 days, fledging in 40–50 days. Single brood. Winter roosts may contain thousands of birds.

HOOPOE *Upupa epops*

- Passage migrant, regular in small numbers in spring, less frequent in autumn, on south, south-east and south-west coasts and on east coast as far north as Norfolk. Rare elsewhere in Great Britain. Open woodland, orchards, parkland.
- Feeds mainly on ground, often close to human habitation, probing on lawns for insect larvae, etc. Does not often come to bird station, but might do so if mealworm/caterpillars/ant pupae were made available in dish. Not shy.
- Normally breeds in Eurasia, but occasionally a hoopoe will nest in one of the southern coastal counties, choosing tree holes, crevices and holes in rough stone walls and ruins.
- Nestbox: Uses them on the continent, presumably may do so here. Enclosed, with 6cm (2½in) entrance hole, interior depth 25cm (10in), floor 15 × 15cm (6 × 6in).
- Clutch: 5–8 whitish-grey or yellowish-olive. May and June. Incubation 18 days; fledging 20–27 days. Two broods.

GREEN WOODPECKER *Picus viridis*

- Resident but local in England and Wales, rare in Scotland, none in Ireland. Deciduous woods, parks and farmland. May discover a sympathetic garden first by finding ant colonies exposed by saturated lawns in a wet winter.
- Searches for insect larvae over tree trunks and branches, probing with long mobile tongue; also feeds freely on ground, especially where there are ants' nests. (Watch out for its droppings – they look like cigarette ends.) In times of hard frost, when ant hills are frozen solid, it may damage beehives by boring holes to reach the insects within. May also attack nestboxes. Will visit bird table for mealworms, bird pudding, etc.
- Nests in tree trunks, choosing soft or rotting timber, boring a hole horizontally 5–7.5cm (2–3in) then descending to make a nest compartment over 30cm (12in) deep and about 15cm (6in) wide at its broadest. A few chips at the bottom form the nest. Sometimes, old holes are used again. Often, starlings take over from them.
- Nestbox: Enclosed type with 6cm (2½in) entrance hole, interior depth 38cm (15in), floor 12.5 × 12.5cm

Green woodpeckers are spectacular red-headed visitors. Males even have a red moustache.

(5 × 5in). Fill with polystyrene chips (which they eject!). Empty box is ideal for starlings.

- Clutch: 5–7 translucent. End of April to May. Incubation 18–19 days; fledging 18–21 days. One brood.

GREAT SPOTTED WOODPECKER *Dendrocopos major*

- Resident, widely distributed in England, central and southern Scotland, none in Ireland. Wooded country – coniferous in north, deciduous in south – hedgerows, orchards and large gardens.
- Hunts over trees for insect larvae, spiders, seeds and nuts, even wedging a nut into a tree crack to deal with it. Will come to bird table for suet especially; also oats, boiled fat bacon, or hanging fat. As adept as tits at feeding upside down and patronizing peanut cages. Also a raider of nestboxes.
- Nests in tree holes 3m (10ft) and higher from ground. A few wood chips form the nest.
- Nestbox: Enclosed type, entrance hole 5cm (2in), interior depth 30cm (12in), floor 12.5cm × 12.5cm (5 × 5in). Fill with polystyrene chips.
- Clutch: 4–7 white eggs. April to June. Incubation 16–18 days; fledging 18–21 days. One brood.

LESSER SPOTTED WOODPECKER *Dendrocopos minor*

Lesser spotted woodpeckers are sparrow-sized and not at all plentiful.

- Sparrow-sized resident in southern England and the Midlands, becoming local and rarer as you get further north. Widely distributed but scattered in Wales. Not in Scotland or Ireland. Same type of country as the great spotted woodpecker.
- An elusive bird, searching upper parts of trees for insect larvae. Will come somewhat nervously and rarely to the garden bird table for fats, nuts and fruit.
- Bores nest hole in decayed soft wood of branch or tree trunk.
- Nestbox: Enclosed, entrance hole 30mm (1¼in), interior depth 30cm (12in), floor 12.5 × 12.5cm (5 × 5in). Fill with polystyrene chips.
- Clutch: 4–6 translucent eggs, early May to mid-June. Incubation 14 days; fledging 21 days. One brood.

SWALLOW *Hirundo rustica*

- Summer resident, generally distributed, much associated with farm buildings. Open farmland, meadows, ponds. Spends much time in flight, especially over water, hunting insects from ground level to 150m (500ft). Unlike swifts, settles freely on buildings and wires. Seldom on ground, except when collecting mud for nest. (Provide muddy puddles in times of drought.)
- Nests inside man-made structures like barns, outhouses, garages (make sure there is permanent access) on rafts and joists, building open mud-and-straw cup, lined with grasses and feathers.
- Nestbox: Improvise a simple saucer shape, or fix half a coconut or a 10 × 10cm (4 × 4in) shallow tray to joist or rafter, even as low as 1.8m (6ft). Will also use specially adapted house martin nestbox placed singly inside building. Or, using an old nest, make a plaster of Paris mould of the interior. Then take potting clay to make a thick replica, complete with fixing flanges or saddles to fit over a joist, remembering that swallows like to nest against something. Remember to allow continuous access to the nest site.
- Clutch: 4–6 eggs, white, spotted with red-brown. April to October. Incubation 14–16 days; fledging about 3 weeks. Two broods, maybe three.

Swifts, house martins and swallows all catch their food in flight, taking insects and even ballooning spiders by open-mouth trawling. Mostly they come to the ground only for nest material. (Swifts don't land on the ground at all – they would find it impossible to get airborne again.)

HOUSE MARTIN *Delichon urbica*

- Summer resident, generally distributed. Habitat as swallow. Hunts insects on the wing, especially over water. Also on the ground.
- Originally a cliff nester, has now adopted buildings. Nests colonially on outside walls, under eaves. Cup shape made of mud gobbets with feathers. In dry summer, provide mud puddles for building materials.
- Nestbox: Artificial nest from suppliers (see page 180). Fix under eaves or high window sill. For best results an existing house martin colony should be close at hand. Prefers to nest on north- and east-facing walls. One nest may work, but the more the merrier. Put them in groups under the horizontal or sloping eaves of houses, barns, etc. The artificial cups are held in position by cup-hooks so that it is possible to slide the nest freely in and out to inspect the contents. The entrance hole should be no more than 25mm (1in) deep, in order to exclude sparrows. Nevertheless, there

have been cases where the hole has been enlarged and sparrows have gained access. One of the objects of using artificial nests is that they frequently encourage house martins to adopt a house not previously 'tenanted' and make their own nests. So even if the boxes are not used, they may be successful in their purpose. Single nests away from an existing colony are susceptible to attack from sparrows. If the birds try to build and the nests fall off the eaves, a series of nails in the facia board may help.

You can easily spot a house martin by its conspicuous white rump.

- It is possible to construct your own artificial nest using Polyfilla or a mixture of cement and sawdust. For a model you can use either a plaster of Paris mould of an old nest or a quarter segment of a plastic ball about 17.5cm (7in) in diameter. The Polyfilla or cement mixture should be smoothed over the model to a thickness of about 8mm (½in), leaving a flange around the edge for fixing. The hole should be cut no deeper than 25mm (1in) and no more than 7.5–10cm (3–4in) wide.

- Occasionally a house martin nest may fall with the young still inside it. The use of a substitute nest may encourage the parents to continue feeding them. A strong deep box so the youngsters cannot fall out placed near the original nest site, is usually successful. If the parents have deserted, or it is not possible to use a substitute nest, then the young must be fed by hand, and if they will not feed by themselves they will have to be force-fed using forceps. Hard-boiled egg yolk mixed with crushed soaked biscuits provides the necessary nutrients. Cut mealworms and maggots make a good food but a little soaked bread must be given occasionally to provide calcium. Feed every two hours, giving 4–6 maggots or a similar amount of egg mixture. The birds should be kept in a warm place. When ready to fly, the best place for them is an aviary where they can practise flying and feeding before release.

- One of the disadvantages is the droppings that will fall beneath the nest. The simplest way to overcome this is to fix up a shelf 25cm (10in) wide about 1.8m (6ft) below the nest, which should catch them. A removable shelf can be made using keyhole brackets. The Wildlife and Countryside Act 1981 makes it an offence intentionally to take, damage or destroy the nest of a house martin (or any bird) while the nest is in use or being built.

- Clutch: 4–5 white eggs. Late April to October. Incubation 14–15 days; fledging 19–21 days. Usually two broods, sometimes three.

PIED WAGTAIL *Motacilla alba*

- Resident and generally distributed. Gardens, farms, buildings and cultivated country.
- Restless bird, feeds over ground for insects, but often flutters up to take one in flight. Fond of shallow pool edges. Will come freely to ground feeding station, scavenging crumbs and scraps where other birds have left unconsidered trifles.
- Nests in holes and on ledges of walls, outhouses, creeper, banks and cliffs. Leaves, twigs, stems, lined with hair, wool and feathers.
- Nestbox: Ledge or open-fronted box, with a floor area of not less than 10 × 10cm (4 × 4in). Fix it in a stone wall, protected by dense cover. Or make a cavity behind a loose stone which can be used as an inspection door.
- Clutch: 5–6 greyish- or bluish-white, spotted grey-brown and grey. Late April to August. Incubation 13–14 days; fledging 14–15 days. Two broods, sometimes three. Often host to cuckoo.

Pied wagtails feed on lawns but also fly up to catch insects.

WAXWING *Bombycilla garrulus*

- Irregular winter visitor, usually to eastern counties.
- Food: Hedgerow berries. May come to bird table for fruit in hard weather. Wide gape engulfs a variety of berries, including holly, ivy, rowan, hips, haws and those of cotoneaster and pyracantha.

DIPPER *Cinclus cinclus*

- Resident, generally distributed in suitable localities. Fast-flowing streams and rivers of hills and mountainous regions.
- Nests in wall and bridge holes, rock faces, tree roots and under waterfalls, always close to fast moving water. Construction of mosses, grasses under an overhang.
- Nestbox: May occasionally occupy an open-fronted robin-type box. A design has been developed to provide nest recesses in the supports of concrete bridges at the time of construction. A recess is left in the concrete mould, by filling it with expanded polystyrene. Once the concrete has nearly set, the entrance hole is chipped out and the polystyrene removed.

- Arrange a suitable perch or dipping stone just above water level if there isn't one already.
- Clutch: About 5 white eggs. End of March. Incubation about 16 days; fledging 19–25 days. Usually two broods.

WREN *Troglodytes troglodytes*

- Resident and widespread. Woodland (preferred) gardens, thickets, woods, rock banks. Avoids the centres of large towns.
- Lives in cracks and crevices, twigs and woodpiles, hedge bottoms, and undergrowth round fallen trees. Active and diligent hunter for insects and spiders. Will take crumbs, but is not a common bird table visitor.
- Nests in hedges, holes in trees, banks or buildings. Male makes several 'cock' nests of moss, grass, leaves, etc. and the hen lines her choice with feathers sometimes weeks after the male built it.
- Nestbox: May take to a hidden tit box, but is much more likely to find a natural or semi-natural place such as a faggot pile or creeper-clad wall. Excavate a cavity in a bundle of pea sticks or brushwood and lean it against a wall. Provide a coil of rope in a shed, or hang up an old coat with capacious pocket.
- Clutch: 5–6 white eggs, spotted with brownish red. March to August. Incubation 14–15 days; fledging 16–17 days. Usually two broods.

Dunnocks tend to be solitary animals, but groups of males may meet to let off steam by aggressive 'wing-waving'. Their sex lives are nothing short of disgraceful. Wife-swapping, three-in-a-bed and mistresses are everyday facts of dunnock life.

DUNNOCK (HEDGE SPARROW)
Prunella modularis

- Resident and generally distributed. Gardens, shrubberies, hedgerows.
- Forages on ground among dead leaves, hedgerow bottoms, etc. Weed seeds in winter, insects in summer. Will come freely to ground station, less readily to bird table for crumbs of cornflakes, cake, biscuit, grated cheese, seeds. Unlike most other birds will eat lentils.
- Nests in hedges and evergreens, faggot heaps. Twigs, moss, leaves, etc., lined with moss, hair and feathers.
- Clutch: 4–5 deep blue eggs. April onward. Incubation 12 days; fledging 12 days. Two broods, sometimes three.

ROBIN *Erithacus rubecula*

- Resident and generally distributed, except in extreme north of Scotland. Gardens, hedgerows, woods with undergrowth.
- Feeds freely in open and in undergrowth. Insects, spiders, worms, weed seeds, fruit berries. Has a flattering relationship with humans and will follow the digging spade hopefully.
- Enthusiastic bird-tabler, very fond of mealworms, will also take seeds, nuts, oats, pudding, etc. Fond of butter and margarine, and is alleged to be able to tell the difference. Unsociable bird, it will endure the close company of its relations at the bird table only in hungry times.
- Nests in gardens and hedgerows, in bankside hollows, tree holes, walls, amongst creeper, on shelves in outbuildings, often at foot of bush or grassy tuft. Foundation of dried leaves and moss, neatly lined with hair and perhaps a feather or two.
- Nestbox: Ledge or tray, open-fronted box. Interior floor at least 10 × 10cm (4 × 4in). Old tin, watering can, or kettle, at least quart-size, well shaded from sun, spout down for drainage. Fix it about 1.5m (5ft) up in a strong fork site, hidden within ivy or other climber. Alternatively inside a shed or barn provided there is access. Prime with a plaited circle of straw.
- Clutch: Usually 5–6 eggs, white with sandy or reddish freckles. Late March to July. Incubation 13–14 days; fledging 12–15 days. Two, sometimes three, even five broods.

Juvenile robins are spotty and lack the red shirt.

BLACKBIRD *Turdus merula*

- Resident and generally distributed. Commonly found in woods, hedges, gardens, shrubberies.
- Feeds in open and in undergrowth, but never far from cover. Makes surprising amount of noise as it searches among dead leaves for insects, worms (which it often steals from a song thrush), fruit, berries and seeds. Will come freely to ground station and to bird table, for sultanas especially, also cheese, fat, apples, cake, Rice Krispies, berries, seeds.
- Nests in hedges, bushes, evergreens, ivy, sometimes in outhouses. Nest is sturdily built of grasses, roots, etc. Inner mud cup lined with grasses.
- Nestbox: Tray or open-fronted box, with a floor area 30 × 30cm (12 × 12in). Or try an inverted cone made of roofing felt. Cut into circle 23cm (9in) in diameter. Cut out and reject a V-shaped sector from centre to a 5cm (2in) arc at periphery. Cut a 25mm (1in) section from centre (to provide drainage). Now overlap open ends 7.5cm (3in) and staple

strongly. Resulting cone is approx 17.5cm (7in) in diameter with a depth of 5cm (2in). Or try a bundle of pea sticks arranged with a central cave.

- Clutch: 4–5 bluish-green eggs, freckled with red-brown. March to September. Incubation 12–15 days; fledging 13–14 days. Two or three broods, the first often being vandalized because it is insufficiently concealed by leaves, later broods being more successful. Five broods have been raised in one season.

FIELDFARE *Turdus pilaris*

- Winter visitor from Scandinavia, generally distributed. Open country, field and hedges, gardens, arriving in Shetland mid-September, Southern England mid-October.
- Flocks feed in open formation across fields, looking for slugs, spiders, insects. In hedgerows, for berries of hawthorn, holly or especially rowan, yew, etc. In hard weather will come to ground station or bird table for berries, windfall fruit, seeds, pudding, etc.
- Breeds in Scandinavia, Central and Eastern Europe and Siberia.

SONG THRUSH *Turdus philomelos*

- Resident and generally distributed. Parks, woods, hedges and gardens, especially around human habitation, but suffering a serious decline for reasons as yet undetermined but possibly related to the use of slug pellets.
- Forages in open and in undergrowth for worms, slugs and snails, which it smashes on 'anvil' stones. Also insects, windfalls, berries and seeds. Will eat soft fruit, but is beneficial on the whole. Somewhat nervous visitor to ground station, not so often on bird table; fond of sultanas, also currants, cheese, fat, apples and scraps.

The song thrush (right) is smaller, shorter and browner than the mistle thrush (left).

- Nests in hedgerows, bushes, trees, among ivy, occasionally in buildings. Nest is strongly built of grasses, roots, etc. Stiffened with mud and with a unique lining of rotten wood or dung mixed with saliva and moulded into shape by the hen's breast. If you want to protect it from magpies, contrive a canopy of chicken wire over nest, but make sure you don't simply make it more obvious to other predators.
- Clutch: 3–5 eggs, blue with greenish tinge, spotted black or red-brown. March to August. Incubation 12–14 days; fledging 13–15 days. Two or three broods.

REDWING *Turdus iliacus*

- Winter visitor, generally distributed, arriving late September onwards. Open country and open woods.
- Feeds in loose flocks in fields or woods. Worms, slugs, snails, insects. Hawthorn, holly, rowan, yew berries. Cotoneaster enthusiast. Will come to ground station or bird table for berries, seeds, fruit in hard weather.
- Breeds in Scandinavia, eastern Europe and Siberia, though a very few nest in Northern Scotland.

MISTLE THRUSH (STORMCOCK) *Turdus viscivorus*

- Resident and generally distributed, except in high mountains and treeless districts. Large gardens, orchards, woods.
- Feeds mainly on ground, although it likes to sing from the highest point of a tree. Thrives on berries and fruit without conflicting with gardener's interests. Yew and rowan especially, but also hawthorn, holly, mistletoe, juniper, rose and ivy. All wild fruits except blackberry. Will come to ground station, less freely to bird table for sultanas, currants, and bird pudding.
- Nests usually in tree fork or on bough. Grasses, moss, etc. Strengthened with earth and lined with fine grasses, the rim ornamented with lichens, bits of wool, feathers, etc.
- Clutch: 4 tawny-cream to greenish-blue eggs, splotched with brown and lilac. February to July. Incubation 13–14 days; fledging 14–16 days. Frequently two broods.

Mistle thrushes will feast on rowan and other berries. They are perfectly capable of bullying a blackbird and may monopolize a food source.

BLACKCAP *Sylvia atricapilla*

- Summer resident, frequently winters, local but fairly distributed, except in remote north and west. Open woodland, thickly bushy places, gardens with trees.
- Active bird, searching in cover for insects, fruit and berries. Not often on ground. Will come to bird table for a wide range of food, including rolled oats, berries, crumbs and scraps, especially in hard weather. Overwintering birds are now relatively common, seen mostly near south coast, south-west peninsula and southern Ireland, relying on garden handouts, even taking peanuts, like tits. They are visitors from Central Europe, while our breeding birds will be leaving for the western

Mediterranean. Windfall apples are an important food item, but they also take cotoneaster, honeysuckle, and holly berries – ivy berries as a last resort. After a heavy snowfall they may take mistletoe berries, rubbing the berry in order to extract the seed. (Apart from thrushes, few birds seem interested in mistletoe berries.)

- Nests in bushes (especially snowberry), hedgerows, evergreens. Stems, roots and grasses, lined with finer grass and hair.
- Clutch: 4–5 eggs, light buff or stone ground, blotched brown and ashy. Mid-May onward. Incubation 10–11 days; fledging 10–13 days. Often two broods.

CHIFFCHAFF *Phylloscopus collybita*

- Summer resident.
- Insectivorous bird, occasional garden visitor in autumn to the bird table for kitchen scraps. Overwintering birds only reluctant garden visitors.

GOLDCREST *Regulus regulus*

Goldcrest (top) is rather dingy by comparison with the brighter firecrest with its orange-red crown.

- Smallest British bird, half the weight of a blue tit. Resident and generally distributed except in remote north-west. Coniferous woodland, gardens, hedgerows.
  - Active and tame bird. Flits from twig to twig searching for spiders and insects. Will come for bread to bird table and to hanging fat.
    - Nests in thick foliage of conifer. Ball of moss lined with feathers, held together by spiders' webs and suspended from branch.
      - Clutch: 7–8 white/ochreous eggs, spotted brown. End April to August. Incubation about 16 days; fledging about 18–20 days. Two broods.

FIRECREST *Regulus ignicapillus*

- A few resident in the south, this gem is more likely to be discovered during autumn migration along the coastline.
  - Habits more or less as goldcrest. Will occasionally take suet or fat from crevices in tree-bark, etc. Has taken bread crumbs from bird table.
  - Nests in tree- or wall-holes; a loose nest of leaves, bark and mosses, lined with hair and feathers.
  - Nestbox: May use tit box.
  - Clutch: 5–9 white, speckled-brown eggs, late May. Incubation 12–13 days; fledging about 13 days. Single brood.

SPOTTED FLYCATCHER *Muscicapa striata*

- Summer resident, generally distributed. Gardens, parks, woodland edges.
- Sits on an exposed perch, flits out frequently to hawk after flying insects.
- Nests against wall or on small ledge supported by creeper or fruit trees, etc. Moss and grass, lined with wool, hair or feathers.
- Nestbox: Ledge or open-fronted box with at least 7.5 × 7.5cm floor. Likes a clear view, so front wall only 25mm high, enough to retain nest. Hide one of those bowl-shaped wire flower baskets in dense honeysuckle, primed with some moss. Have a perch not far away.
- Clutch: 4–5 greenish-grey, with brown spots. Mid-May to June. Incubation 12–14 days; fledging 12–15 days. One brood, maybe two.

Both the spotted and the pied flycatcher use the same technique, watching silently from a perch before leaping out to catch insects in flight or on the ground.

LONG-TAILED TIT *Aegithalos caudatus*

- Resident and generally distributed except in very barren districts and islands. Thickets, bushy heaths and hedgerows. Also woods in winter.
- Feeds in trees, sometimes on ground, restlessly searching for insects and seeds. Sociable parties visit gardens and bird tables for suet, pudding, bread crumbs, grated cheese, etc., especially in hard weather. Peanut enthusiasts once they get the taste.
- Nests in bushes, furze or brambles, sometimes in trees. Large egg-shaped nest of moss woven with cobwebs and hair with a lining of many feathers. Entrance hole near top.
- Clutch: 7–12 eggs, sometimes unmarked, sometimes a cap of spots or freckles. March–April. Incubation 14–18 days; fledging 15–16 days. Normally one brood.

MARSH TIT *Parus palustris*

- Resident and widespread in most of England and Wales, but not Scotland or Ireland. Deciduous woods, hedgerows, thickets and sometimes in gardens. Likes to be near broad-leafed woodland and not, as might reasonably be imagined from its name, in marshes.
- Forages over trees for insects; on ground for weed seeds, beechmast, berries and sunflower seeds. Comes to bird table and hanging devices for food as blue tit.

- Nests in holes in willows, alders, sometimes in walls. Moss with lining of hair or down.
- Nestbox: As blue tit.
- Clutch: 6–8 white eggs, spotted red-brown. End April and May. Incubation 13 days; fledging 16–18 days. Generally one brood.

WILLOW TIT *Parus montanus*

- Resident, but in fast decline. Fairly frequent in parts of south-east England, scattered locally elsewhere. Marshy or damp woods, conifers, hedges and thickets.
- Forages over trees and on ground for insects, spiders and berries. Will come to bird table for seeds, peanuts.
- Excavates a nest chamber in soft rotten wood – usually birch, willow, alder or elder. Pad of down mixed with wood-fibre, some feathers.
- Nestbox: As for blue tit, but not enthusiastic. Stuff it full of sawdust or polystyrene chips so that the willow tit has to excavate a hole. But a far more successful method is to get a rotten silver birch or alder trunk about 1.8m (6ft) long and 12.5 or 15 cm (5 or 6in) in diameter, and strap it to a convenient tree, allowing the bird to finish the job. Cap the top with polythene so that rain cannot penetrate easily. It seems that the presence of a suitable rotten tree which they can excavate is all that is needed to attract them to breed in an area they visit during winter. Nests are usually between 60cm and 1.5m (2–5ft) high, averaging 90cm (3ft), so place the trunk accordingly. Birch is the preferred site, alder and elder come as a poor second choice.
- Clutch: 6–9 white eggs, spotted brown-red. Late April and May. Incubation 13 days; fledging 17–19 days. Probably one brood.

CRESTED TIT *Parus cristatus*

- Resident in a few parts of north-east Scotland only. Mostly found in pine forests and woods.
- Forages mainly on tree trunks for insects, ripe pine cone seeds, berries. Will come to feed at tit-bell and, sometimes patronize peanut cages.
- Nests in holes or crevices in decayed pine stumps, also in alders and birches and sometimes in fencing posts. Dead moss lined with hair of deer or hare, sometimes feathers or wool.
- Nestbox: Enclosed with 30–38mm (1⅛–1½in) entrance hole, interior depth not less than 12.5cm (5in), floor not less than 10 × 10cm (4 × 4in).

From top – coal, marsh and willow tit. Coal tit is easy, with the white patch at the back of the head. Confusingly, marsh is typical of trees and woodland. Willow is slimmer, a bird of a variety of woodland and damp woodland areas in the breeding season. Best separated by song, marsh sneezes pitchoo, willow is a weaker, quiet buzzing. Marsh tit has glossy black cap. No problem, really ...

- Clutch: 5–6 white eggs, splotched with chestnut red. End April and May. Incubation 14–15 days; fledging 17–18 days. One brood.

COAL TIT *Parus ater*

- Resident and generally distributed. Wooded country and gardens with a preference for conifers. Not so commonly found in orchards and hedgerows.
- Forages in trees, especially conifers, for insects and spiders. On ground, for seeds and nuts. Not quite so common at bird tables as great and blue tits, but will take the same foods.
- Nests in tree, wall or bank holes, close to ground. Moss with thick layer of hair or down and feathers.
- Nestbox: As blue tit, but can be close to the ground.
- Clutch: 7–11 white eggs, with reddish-brown spots. Late April and May. Incubation 13–14 days; fledging 16 days. Sometimes two broods.

BLUE TIT *Parus caeruleus*

- Resident and generally distributed except in north-west Scotland. Woodland, hedges, shrubberies.
- Forages in trees, hedgerows and around houses. Eats wheat, nuts, seeds and insects. Damage to buds and ripe fruit outweighed by consumption of insects. Pugnacious, will hold insect prey with its feet and dismember with bill almost like a hawk. Confiding and adaptable species that will come readily to bird feeding stations for almost anything. Hauls peanut strings 'beak over claw' in a version of the natural behaviour involved in pulling leafy twigs closer to inspect for caterpillars. Milk-drinker, as great tit. Blue tits breed most successfully in deciduous woodland, where there is an abundance of caterpillars. Their breeding success is least in built-up areas, even though their clutch sizes are smaller to compensate for the poor food available.
- Nests as great tit. Blue tits may go to a nestbox because the best natural sites have been taken by the dominant great tits.
- Nestbox: Enclosed, with 25mm (1in) entrance hole, otherwise as great tit.
- Clutch: 7–12 eggs (there is a record of 19, probably involving two females), usually spotted light chestnut. Late April and May. Incubation 13–14 days; fledging 15–21 days. One brood.

GREAT TIT *Parus major*

- Resident and generally distributed, scarcer in northern Scotland. Woodland, hedges, gardens.
- Forages in trees and hedgerows for insects, spiders, worms. Fruit, peas, nuts and seeds. Does some damage to buds in spring, but it was once estimated that one pair of great tits will destroy 7000–8000 insects, mainly caterpillars, in about 3 weeks. Fierce bird that will attack and eat a bee. Comes freely to bird table, to hoppers and scrap baskets, where it will display its acrobatic powers as it takes coconut, peanuts, hemp and other seeds, meat, fat, suet, pudding and cheese.
- Nests in tree or wall holes, or crevices. Also in secondhand nests, or the foundations of larger nests. If no natural sites are available, it may use letterboxes, flower pots, beehives and almost any kind of hole. Nest lined with a thick layer of hair or down.
- Nestbox: Enclosed, with 29mm (1⅛in) diameter entrance hole or slightly larger, interior depth at least 12.5 cm (5in) from hole to floor, and floor at least 10 × 10 cm (4 × 4in). Do not have any perch on the outside of the box. Make sure there is an open flight path for their final approach and that there is no easy access for cats. Great tits are the most enthusiastic customers for boxes, with blue tits coming second. They not uncommonly occupy the same box, the great tits taking over, covering the blue tits' eggs with a fresh lining and hatching only their own eggs (though mixed broods are not unknown). Tit boxes are successful even in woodland, if there is a shortage of old trees because management procedures do not tolerate them. The result is a strong competition for suitable sites.
- Clutch: 5–12 white eggs, splotched reddish-brown. End April to June. Incubation 12–16 days; fledging 18–24 days. One brood, occasionally two.

Great tits are the largest of the tits. In aggressive display, the dominant bird holds his head high and bares his black breast-stripe to intimidate his opponent.

NUTHATCH *Sitta europaea*

- Resident and fairly common in Wales and southern England. Mature broad-leafed woodland, old trees, parkland, gardens.
- Dodges about on tree trunks. Wedges nuts, acorns, beechmast and seeds in crevices, and hacks them open with bill. Also takes insects. Will come freely to bird table and hanging devices for hemp, seeds, nuts, cake, fat,

etc. Try jamming a brazil nut into a crevice. May carry off peanuts and hoard them in a cache.

- Nests in tree holes or sometimes in holes in walls. Female fills crevice and reduces entrance to desired size with mud. Lines nest with bark flakes or leaves.
- Nestbox: Enclosed, with 32mm (1¼in) or larger entrance hole, interior depth not less than 12.5cm (5in), floor not less than 10 × 10cm (4 × 4in).
- Clutch: 5–9 white eggs, spotted with red-brown. End April to June. Incubation 14–15 days; fledging about 24 days. One brood, occasionally two.

TREECREEPER *Certhia familiaris*

Treecreepers are well named.

- Resident and generally distributed. Woodland, parks, gardens with large trees.
- Forages unobtrusively in mouse-like fashion for insects over trees. Does not come freely to bird table, but may indulge in crushed nuts, porridge or suet fat spread in crevices of rough-barked trees, especially *Wellingtonia*. Has visited peanut feeders, possibly in increasing numbers. Try putting out uncooked pastry. May take fat from a hanging container.
- Nests behind loose bark or cracks on tree trunks, or behind ivy. Sometimes in wall or building crevices. Twigs, moss, grass, lined with feathers and bits of wool.
- Nestbox: May come to conventional enclosed type, but a wedge-shaped box has been specially designed with their needs in mind, though I've had one up for years without success. An alternative design involves a book-shaped box 18cm (7¼in) tall by 12 × 4cm (4¾ × 1⁹⁄₁₆in), with a 5 × 2.5cm (2 × 1in) entrance hole at the top of the 'spine'. Clamp it to a tree trunk at around 3m (10ft) high. Or try securing a loose piece of bark to a tree trunk to simulate a natural crevice. Entrance must be alongside tree trunk, in a way which allows the bird to 'sidle' into the cavity.
- Clutch: 5–6 usually white eggs, with red-brown spots at larger end. End April to June. Incubation 14–15 days; fledging 14–15 days. There may be a second brood.

JAY *Garrulus glandarius*

- Resident and generally distributed. Woodland, never far from trees.
- Hops about branches and on ground. Mostly vegetable food, peas, potatoes, corn, beechmast, nuts, fruit and berries. Animal food includes

eggs and small birds, mice, slugs, snails, worms and insects. Eats large numbers of acorns and, like other crows, has the habit of burying acorns and other surplus food in secret places in trees and under ground. Shy bird, except in some well-timbered suburban areas where it becomes very tame and will come to the bird table or ground station for almost any food.

- Nests fairly low in undergrowth or tree-fork. Sticks and twigs and a little earth, lined with roots and perhaps hair.
- Clutch: 5–6 sage-green or olive-buff eggs, mottled with darker olive spots. Early May. Incubation 16–17 days; fledging 20 days. One brood.

MAGPIE *Pica pica*

- Resident and generally distributed in England and Wales, scarce in parts of Scotland. Farmland and open country with hedges and trees; suburbs and urban areas.
- Frequently in pairs or small parties foraging on ground and in hedgerows mainly for small mammals, insects, cereals, fruit, nuts, peas and berries. Will come to bird table or ground station for large scraps, which it takes away. Suffers from an exaggerated public perception of its impact on small bird populations, which is much less than popularly believed. A BTO analysis of data showed that songbird numbers were no different in areas of high magpie concentration than in other places where there were few. It found no link between increased magpie numbers and declines in songbirds. When the magpie eats eggs or small birds it is doing its job as a magpie, not acting like a pantomime villain! Nests in tall trees, thorny bush or neglected hedgerow. Bulky, domed structure of sticks, with an inner lining of earth and roots.
- Clutch: 5–8 eggs, greenish-blue to yellowish and greyish-green, spotted and mottled brown and ash. April onwards. Incubation 17–18 days; fledging about 22–27 days. One brood.

JACKDAW *Corvus monedula*

- Resident and common except in north-west Scotland. Farm and parkland, cliffs, old buildings.
- Jaunty bird, feeding in parties or flocks on animal and vegetable matter. Will take young birds and eggs if it gets the chance. Comes freely to bird table or ground station for scraps, cereals, potato, fruit, berries and nuts. Fond of macaroni cheese.
- Nests in colonies in trees, buildings, rocks or rabbit burrows, holes, cracks

or crevices. Almost any hole will do – often in bottom of rook or heron's nest. Twigs, sometimes very bulky, sometimes not. Lining of grass, wool, hair, etc.

- Nestbox: Enclosed type, with not less than 15cm (6in) entrance hole, 43cm (17in) interior depth, and at least a 19 × 19cm (7½ × 7½in) floor. Or open type as for kestrel.
- Clutch: Usually 4–6 pale greenish-blue, spotted brownish black. Mid-April. Incubation 17–18 days; fledging 30–35 days. One brood.

STARLING *Sturnus vulgaris*

- Resident and generally distributed. Successfully adapted to human ways, but in serious decline, possibly related to changes in grassland management. Needs friends, suffers from an unjustified reputation as 'greedy'.
- Active bird, foraging on ground and in trees and hawking for insects. Animal and vegetable foods of almost any kind. Enthusiastic bird table and ground station visitor. Sometimes defeated by hanging devices, but has learnt to extract peanuts from cages. Very fond of leg-of-lamb bones, particularly marrow, but will eat anything available.
- Nests, often in colonies, in tree or building holes. Untidy structure of straw and grasses lined with feathers.
- Nestbox: Enclosed, with entrance hole 5cm (2in) diameter, inside depth 30cm (12in), floor area 23 × 23cm (9 × 9in).

Both parent starlings have to work hard to find enough insects to feed a noisy family of maybe nine young.

- Starlings will explore many possibilities of piracy, and will sometimes take over an old tit box, when the wood has softened enough to enable them to hack away at the hole and enlarge it.
- Clutch: 4–7, maybe more nowadays, pale blue eggs. End of March onwards. (They often get taken short and lay one on the lawn.) Incubation 12–13 days; fledging 20–22 days. Usually one brood, sometimes two in south-east England.

HOUSE SPARROW *Passer domesticus*

- Resident and widely distributed except in the remote Scottish Highlands but in severe decline. Cultivated land and vicinity of human habitation. In the past was very successful; sadly this is no longer the case. Various

Some confusing females. From the top – house sparrow, plain open faced, pale eyebrow, plain brown cap. Bull-necked greenfinch – dull grey/green colours. Heavy set head with stout bill. Reed bunting – stripey with dark moustache, brown ear-coverts, pale yellow ochre eyebrow, two tone brown cap.

theories for cause of decline, but none conclusive. Even so, it is still a common visitor to some feeding stations.

■ Operates in non-territorial 'gangs', cleaning up wherever there are easy pickings on farms, hedgerows, parks, gardens, docks, railways, and 'waste' land of all kinds. Corn, seeds, insects. Tough customer at the bird table, eating almost anything, especially cereal-based foods. Wastes a great deal. Has learned to extract peanuts from net bags, sometimes even hovering to do so. May hang upside-down tit-style to get at nuts from a 'difficult' feeder.

■ Nests in holes or niches around occupied houses: eaves, drainpiping, creeper, also in hedges and trees, house martins' nests, or in the foundations of rooks' nests. Untidy structure of straw and grasses lined with feathers and oddments. In cramped locations may consist of lining only. Once established, the pair will remain together, faithful to their nest site which the cock bird will defend.

■ Nestbox: Enclosed, with entrance hole 32mm (1¼in) diameter, inside depth not less than 12.5cm (5in), floor area 15 × 15cm (6 × 6in). Fix it a couple of metres high in an undisturbed place. As sociable nesters, they may be keen on the new terrace designs of nestbox, though this is disputed.

■ Clutch: 3–6 blueish-white eggs, finely spotted grey and brown. May to August. Incubation 9–18 days; fledging 11–19 days. One to four broods.

TREE SPARROW *Passer montanus*

■ Resident and widely distributed in England, Wales, eastern side of Scotland and a few parts of Ireland. 'Country cousin' of house sparrow, frequenting same habitat but less attached to human habitations. Has been in serious decline, just possibly due for recovery.

■ Feeds on weed seeds, corn, insects, spiders. Will visit bird table for seeds and scraps but is a shy bird compared with the house sparrow.

■ Nests in holes of trees, banks, haystacks and thatch, buildings and in foundations of disused rook or magpie nests. Untidy, similar to that of house sparrow.

■ Nestbox: Enclosed, with entrance hole 28mm (1⅛in) diameter, inside depth not less than 15cm (6in), floor not less than 10 × 10cm (4 × 4in). Very susceptible to disturbance.

■ Clutch: 5–7, smaller, browner, darker than those of house sparrow. Late April to August. Incubation 12–14 days; fledging 12–14 days. One brood, occasionally two or even three.

The chaffinch is the commonest finch. Its song – chip, chip, chip, chip, tissee chweeo – is said to display subtle dialect characteristics.

CHAFFINCH *Fringilla coelebs*

- Resident and widely distributed. Gardens, hedgerows, woods, commons, farmland.
- Forages on ground and in trees. Insects, spiders, fruit, fruit buds. Tame and enthusiastic bird-tabler, taking seeds of all kinds, bird pudding, scraps and berries.
- Nests in hedgerows, orchards, gardens, not choosy. Beautiful structure of moss with interwoven grass and roots, decorated with lichens held together by spiders' webs. Lined with hair and feathers.
- Clutch: 4–5 greenish-blue to brownish-stone eggs, spotted/streaked purplish-brown. Mid-April to June. Incubation 11–13 days; fledging 13–14 days. Mostly single-brooded.

BRAMBLING *Fringilla montifringilla*

- Largely a winter visitor to Great Britain. Has been known to take mixed seeds dropped from bird table and peanuts from a mesh bag. Visits bird table in hard weather, or when beechmast crop fails.

GREENFINCH *Carduelis chloris*

- Resident and common. Gardens, shrubberies, farmland.
- Feeds sociably on ground and in trees. Seeds of all kinds, berries, fruit tree buds, occasionally beetles, ants, aphids. Comes to bird table and seed hoppers for sunflower seed especially, but is also enthusiastic about peanuts. Will appear where not previously seen when peanut bag hoisted. Will even eat buckwheat. Berries of yew, ivy, hawthorn, elder, etc. Windfalls.
- Nests in hedgerows and evergreen bushes and trees. Moss interwoven with twigs and lined with roots and hair, sometimes feathers.
- Clutch: 4–6 eggs, ground colour dirty white to pale greenish-blue, variably spotted red-brown. Late April/May onwards. Incubation 13–14 days; fledging 13–16 days. Two broods, sometimes three.

GOLDFINCH *Carduelis carduelis*

- Resident and generally distributed. Gardens, orchards and cultivated land.
- Small flocks flitter around plant seed-heads, not so much on the ground. Seeds, especially of thistles, teasel and other weeds. Also insects. Increasingly common at the bird table and tube feeders for small seeds, especially niger, offered in the specially designed tube feeder. Crack some hemp for them, as their beaks are not so strong as those of other finches. They will patronize peanut cages. Spring feeding, for instance with the specially designed niger tube-feeder, is important.
- Nests especially in fruit trees and chestnuts. Also in hedges and thick berberis. Elegant nest of roots, grass, moss and lichens, lined with vegetable down and wool, placed far out at the end of the branch.
- Clutch: 5–6 bluish-white eggs, spotted and streaked red-brown. Early May onwards. Incubation 12–13 days; fledging 13–15 days. Two broods, sometimes three.

SISKIN *Carduelis spinus*

- Resident in parts of Ireland, Scotland and Wales and in Devon, the New Forest and Norfolk. Increasing. Mainly winter visitor, widely distributed. Woods in summer, otherwise copses, streams, gardens.
- Seen in mixed parties with redpolls searching spruce, birch and larch for seeds. Since the mid-1960s has become increasingly common in gardens in winter, a habit that spread from Surrey through the south-east. Perhaps first attracted by suitable seed-bearing trees, it has stayed to enjoy the bird table, specializing in meat fat and peanuts. Very tame, seeming almost indifferent to people, though aggressive in behaviour to other birds. Said to be especially attracted to peanuts in red mesh bags; though one observer found that while red mesh failed, nuts in a white RSPB scrap cage did the trick. (Mesh bags are not recommended.)
- Nests in conifers, high up. Moss and wool interwoven with grass and twigs. Lined with rootlets, down and feathers.
- Clutch: 4–5 eggs. April to May. Incubation 11–12 days; fledging about 15 days. Two broods.

REDPOLL *Acanthis flammea*

- Grain-eater, may come to bird table for kitchen scraps, especially in Scotland.

CROSSBILL *Loxia curvirostra*

- Late summer visitor. Varying numbers. Every few years invades and over-winters in great numbers, many individuals remaining to breed. Coniferous woods, gardens and parks. Clambers about branches parrot-fashion in parties, wrenching off pine and larch cones. Holds cone in one foot while it splits the scales and extracts the seed with its tongue. Apart from cone seeds, will eat thistle seeds, berries and insects. Very tame, it will visit bird table for seeds, especially sunflower. Very fond of water and bathing.
- Nests on pine branches. Foundation of twigs, cups of moss, grass and wool lined with grass, fur, hair, feathers.
- Clutch: 4 greenish-white eggs with few spots/streaks of purple-red. January to July. Incubation 12–13 days; fledging more than 24 days. One brood.

BULLFINCH *Pyrrhula pyrrhula*

- Resident and generally distributed. Shrubberies, copses, gardens, orchards, hedgerows.
- In autumn and early winter eats mainly weed seeds, some berries; in a hard winter, if its natural food, ashmast, is short it will ravage fruit tree buds. Not keen on bird tables, may occasionally come for seeds and berries, but is especially fond of black and red rape. Will take peanuts from a mesh bag (or another bird), but cannot extract them from shell.
- Nests in hedges, evergreen bushes, creeper, brambles. Foundation of twig and moss, cup lined with interlacing roots and hair.
- Clutch: 4–6 green-blue eggs with few purple-brown spots and streaks. Late April onwards. Incubation 12–14 days; fledging 12–17 days. Two broods, maybe three.

HAWFINCH *Coccothraustes coccothraustes*

- Resident, generally distributed, but not much in evidence; local in Britain, but very rare in Ireland. Woodland, parks, orchards and wooded gardens, especially where there is hornbeam.
- Feeds in trees, taking kernels and seeds. Fond of green peas. Will come shyly to bird table for fruit, seeds and nuts. Highly-developed bill muscles enable it to crack cherry and plum stones, etc., to extract the kernel.
- Nests on fruit tree branches or in bushes and other trees. Foundation of twigs supports shallow cup of lichens, moss, grass lined thinly with roots and hair.

- Clutch: 4–6 eggs, ground colour light bluish or greyish-green spotted and streaked blackish-brown. Late April onwards. Incubation about 9 days; fledging 10–11 days. Occasionally two broods.

SNOW BUNTING *Plectrophenax nivalis*

- Has patronized Scottish bird tables in winter (and vessels of the Royal Navy in northern latitudes!).

YELLOWHAMMER (YELLOW BUNTING) *Emberiza citrinella*

- Resident and generally distributed. Farmland with hedgerows or bush cover, bushy commons and heaths. Nowadays less common along roadsides.
- Feeds mainly on ground, hopping and pecking for corn, weed seeds, wild fruits (including blackberries, which most birds don't like), leaves, grasses. Insects, spiders, worms, etc. Will come to scattered 'special mix' type seed or to a garden seed-hopper once it has discovered it (as will cirl bunting, incidentally), but not an enthusiastic garden bird.
- Nests in bottom of hedgerow or bush. Straw, grass, stalks, moss-lined with hair and grass.
- Clutch: 3–5 eggs, whitish to purplish to brownish-red with dark brown hairlines and spots. Late April onwards. Incubation 12–14 days; fledging 12–13 days. Two or three broods.

Snow buntings are common birds of the Arctic tundra yet a few dozen breed in northern Britain while some ten thousand or so winter here and around the north-west and east coasts.

REED BUNTING *Emberiza schoeniclus*

- Resident and generally distributed except in Shetlands, but declining. Reedbeds, rushy pastures, marginal land and hedgerows, having recently added dry country and suburbia to its ancestral wetland habitat.
- In wintertime joins with yellowhammers and finches in open fields and visits gardens, often in early spring, for seeds and crushed oats.
- Nests in marshy ground, with thick vegetation, sometimes in bushes. Dried grasses and moss, lined with fine grasses, hair.
- Nestbox: May take advantage of goose/duck raft and nest on it.
- Clutch: 4–5 bluish eggs. April/May. Incubation about 13–14 days; fledging 10–13 days. Two, maybe three broods.

Mammals

Birds are comparatively easy to see. They may not always sit still for long enough to be identified, but at least we know that they are there – most of them are active during the daytime; we get a glimpse of plumage; hear a snatch of song. Most mammals, by contrast, keep a much lower profile, but they will still share our gardens and we can help to encourage them.

Night meets day

Dawn is a good time to do your garden-wildlife watching. The nocturnal animals are finishing their night's work and now is your best chance to see foxes, badgers, rabbits and hedgehogs before they retire. And now is the time for diurnal birds to wake up and sing to proclaim a new day. There are fewer people about, and less human disturbance means more wildlife to be seen. Early risers like blackbirds, thrushes and robins are up for the worms, just as the hedgehog and badger are having a late-night snack before retiring for the day. Slug-a-bed birds are late risers for perfectly good reasons: until the warmth of the sun starts some air-rising thermals going there's not much action from flying insects. Swallows and swifts and martins stay in bed late, but soon enough the new shift takes over.

Come into the garden, Maud,
For the black bat, night, has flown.
Alfred, Lord Tennyson (1809–1892)

Squirrels tend to be active throughout the day, but for most wild mammals, their peak of activity tends to be during the twilight hours. Many also keep an even lower profile by hibernating for the winter months when food is scarce and difficult to find. However, as the year progresses try sitting quietly in your garden or by your wildlife-watching window as dusk falls on a spring or summer's evening – you never know what you might see.

Hedgehogs

The hedgehog is a welcome visitor, with his carefree shuffling and scrunching around the shrubbery and borders. Everyone's favourite, he is the most welcome wild inhabitant of a garden. He eats mainly insects, insect larvae and worms. No bad habits, no trouble,

Hedgehog hotel. Hogs need a plentiful supply of dry leaves and a suitable winter nest site. If you provide a nestbox, put it in an undisturbed area of the garden and be sure there's lots of bedding close by.

easy to identify, prickly by coat but not by character, he is abundant in suburban areas, especially around old houses and unkempt gardens. Garden life suits him, food prospects are good and predators few. Quite apart from their engaging habits, hedgehogs are positively useful. They eat formidable quantities of slugs, millipedes and caterpillars, but not useful insects such as ladybirds, devil's coach-horses and violet ground-beetles.

Along with the mole and the shrews he is a representative of the Insectivora, an order of mammals which feeds mainly on insects. So he is not a fast-mover, and although he has good teeth he doesn't make a great deal of use of them in defence. Faced with an attacker, he simply curls up to hide his face and his soft underbelly and erects his sharp spines as a prickly and impenetrable barrier. And a very effective defence it must be, to judge from the nonchalant way the animal chunters its way round the leafy borders of the garden. But this technique comes sadly adrift when, as so often happens, he is discovered in the roadway by the headlights of a car. Rolling up, instead of running off, he risks being flattened.

A hedgehog is a noisy hunter, snuffling and grunting, sniffing and scenting with a disregard for peace and quiet, yet with very sensitive moist nose-membranes, which smell out the food possibilities. He turns over leaves and mosses, grubbing about. A loud and vulgar snort may greet the discovery of a toothsome morsel like a snail. And then, as you would by now expect, he proceeds to eat it on the spot with noisy enjoyment, snap, crackle and pop. Woodlice, slugs and worms, scraps from the bird table, he relishes them all. But he needs a big garden to sustain him, or he will climb walls like a born mountaineer and forage next door as well. Many people cherish him, putting out dishes of minced meat and egg, milk and cheese; he never seems wild about minced meat, his plebeian taste is well pleased with a slice of factory bread and a piece of fruit cake! However, the experts advise not to offer milk, which can cause digestive upsets, and suggest that if you want to supplement his diet, a little tinned dog or cat food will suffice. Special hedgehog food is also available from some garden wildlife suppliers.

If you frighten him by appearing suddenly he will jump sideways and erect his spines, possibly curling up, but as often as not he will ignore you in a lordly manner and allow you to join him in the hunt. Over a period you will find it easy to tame him. Slow but sure is the rule. Don't stare him in the face, move quietly but freely. Feed him regularly, and if you can afford mealworms that will accelerate the process.

On midsummer nights on the open lawn you may see the bucolic courtship of the hedgehogs, where one partner circles round and round the other for what seems like hours. The nest will be made against tree roots, in a compost heap or woodpile or in brambles. It is made of grass and leaves, in the form of a mound. Then the hog burrows into it and shapes a hollow chamber. A most interesting design for a hedgehog nestbox has been developed by the Henry Doubleday Research Association, now known as Garden Organic. The box should be about 10 × 38 × 12.5cm (4 × 13 × 5in) high, and made of untreated timber (hedgehogs have a keen sense of smell, objecting to both tobacco smoke and artificial preservatives). To prevent cats getting in, there should be an entrance tunnel, 60cm (2ft) long and with a 10 × 10cm (4 × 4in) square section.

It is important that there should be a ventilation shaft, and that air should be able to pass freely through the box; otherwise it will become uncomfortably wet inside. Bear in mind that the hedgehog will probably try to fill the box very full with hay, so try to construct the box so that the ventilation pipe does not get blocked. The box needs to be rainproof so cover the roof with a piece of polythene that just overlaps the sides of the box. (Do not seal the box completely with polythene or there will be condensation and the inside of the box will become sodden before its time). Cover the whole assembly with at least 30cm (12in) of earth, so that just the entrance tunnel and feeding hatch are visible. Hedgehogs like to have plenty of dry bedding in their homes, so make some hay or dry leaves available near the entrance.

Hedgehog diet is almost entirely of ground-level invertebrates, though they may take bird's eggs or chicks if they get the chance. They certainly enjoy slugs. In folklore, and perhaps in fact, they carry apples on their spines and suck milk from cows.

The young hedgehogs are born blind, their spines are soft and white but soon superseded by the familiar dark ones, which harden slowly over a period of weeks.

The first litter may be born in May or June, leaving the nest in July, but there is often a second. There is no more charming sight than an adult hedgehog leading a caravan of young ones about the garden as they learn the trade.

Moles

Worms are blind and deaf, but very sensitive to vibrations. The approach of a mole may send them post-haste to the surface to face the birds. If you are ever fortunate enough to see a mole at work, or rather to see a molehill erupting as a result of the unseen mole's efforts, watch closely to see if worms erupt as well as a result of the bad vibes. If the underground vibrations of an approaching mole may cause the worm to surface, perhaps the act of thumping the ground from above may have the same effect: that explains why we so often see rooks and gulls paddling up and down, walking hard on the same spot. Perhaps the vibrations do the trick, or perhaps the collapse of the soil structure deprives the worm of air. Whatever the reason, there's no doubt that this is a successful worming technique for the crow family and for gulls.

Moles the crumbled Earth in Hillocks raise.

John Gay (1685–1732)

Living a subterranean existence, the mole has small eyes and very poor eyesight, but makes up with extra sensitivity to touch and vibration, feeling his way along in the dark with great aplomb. You may never have actually set eyes on one, but you can hardly have missed the evidence that moles are about.

Those neat little piles of spoil earth have caused a lot of aggro to bowlers, cricketers and lawn obsessives, so for all his reticence the mole is a much persecuted beast. At one time there was a price on his warm velvety coat, when countrymen wore moleskin trousers, but now he pays the price simply for offending our sense of tidiness. His best chance of a quiet life is when he sets up home in woodland where his mounds are lost among the bracken and the litter of dead wood and leaves.

His down-to-earth name comes from the Old English word molde – dust – so we have moldewarp, the earth-thrower. He naturally prefers light loose soil, even though that may produce fewer worms, but he is provided with powerful tools for his trade. To make passage easier, his appendages are somewhat on the short side, but the forelegs are built like a navvy's, with hands which scrape and lever him through the soil, aided by his equally powerful neck muscles.

Mini-mammals

Mice, voles and shrews are integral parts of a garden, but they generally keep a very low profile, literally hugging the ground, if not entirely under it. Shrews are insectivorous and have to eat almost continuously; voles and mice may not be so welcome as they eat roots of plants and seeds, but in their turn they provide food for birds such as kestrels and owls. Population studies of small mammals have indicated that limiting factors on wood mice were the presence of domestic cats and the distance to the nearest patch of natural or seminatural vegetation. Gardens of the right quality might offset the effects of habitat fragmentation.

Bats

I suppose the most misunderstood and almost the least welcome wild neighbour is the bat. It is not a flying mouse, for all the flittermouse name, but belongs to a group called 'hand-wings', Chiroptera. Bats have a short thumb with a curved claw, used as a grappling iron when climbing. Their other fingers are long and the double skin that stretches over them forms their wings. There are seventeen species of bat in Britain; most of them either rare or confined to particular areas; the one you are most likely to see is the smallest, the pipistrelle.

Other mammals may glide or parachute, but bats are master aviators capable of true powered flight. They roost in various places, according to species, but very often in buildings, preferring a clean and draught-free place, so you find them often enough in a fairly new, dust-free and non-cobwebby house. But they are not especially faithful to one particular roosting place and may move away from time to time. Apart from hollow trees, they may choose a cave or quarry, roofs, attics or church towers for instance. Once inside, they hang themselves upside down from the roof where they feel safe. The numbers in a summer breeding colony may be in the hundreds, but a few dozens are more usual. Their droppings may accumulate on the floor, but they are unobjectionable, being unsmelly, dry and non-corrosive. On the whole I think they just improve the insulation of the house and save you a bit on your electricity bill. Bats are much maligned creatures which are much more likely to decimate the flying insects round your house than get tangled in your hair. There might be a faint hint of truth in that old story, because it could happen, but the poor bat would be anxious to get out as quickly as possible and would certainly not be going to suck your blood.

Happily, all bats and their roosting sites are now protected by law, so if you are concerned about bats roosting in your attic, or need to treat your timber for woodworm, you must contact the

Especially at dusk, screaming parties of swifts dash wildly about the rooftops. Sharp eyes may see a true nocturnal hunter below – a long-eared bat.

relevant statutory nature conservation
organization, such as English Nature, for
advice before carrying out any sort of work.
I try hard to persuade people to tolerate
these absolutely harmless creatures which
face enough problems already. Their
numbers are sadly declining, for various
reasons including cave disturbance, rubbish
dumping and ill-advised roof fumigation.
As bats are finding it more and more
difficult to find suitable roost places, it is
a kindly gesture to provide potential sites
for them. If you have a suitable roof or loft
space, make sure there is an entrance hole.
Or you might try fixing a piece of boarding
to one of your walls by way of 20mm (¾in)
battens, thus offering the sort of secret space
bats might adopt. If the wood is warping, so
much the better, since it will produce its own
splits for access. Remember the seasonal requirements:
summer warmth for nurseries, winter stability for hibernation,
in choosing a site. Make sure there is some sun, but not too much.

*A tree-hole or crevice
offers a roost place
for many bat species,
including this
pipistrelle.*

Bat boxes make a change from tit boxes for the birds, and of course
there is no reason why you should not offer both. In fact bat boxes
offer the same facilities as do tit boxes, in other words they provide an
alternative to a hole in a tree. But whereas tit boxes are used primarily
for nesting, and may serve as roost boxes out of the breeding season,
the function of the bat box is exactly the opposite. Although they
might be used for breeding, they are very much more likely to be used
for straightforward roosting. And the other great difference from the
conventional bird box is in the entrance hole. For the bats like to gain
access by way of a slit at the bottom of the box.

The shape and size of your bat box are not critical, but it is easiest
and most convenient to build a bird box shape; the interior distance
from front to back should not exceed 10cm (4in), for bats prefer a
constricted space. Use rough-sawn and untreated 25mm (1in)
planking, which you further roughen by making shallow horizontal
sawcuts both inside and out (unlike birds, bats crawl about all over the
box, both sides!). The entrance slit should be 15–20mm (½–¾in) wide

British bats hunt by echolocation, finding prey by shouting at them and then analysing the echo. Noctules have broad wings, they chase insects over pasture and within dense vegetation, able to fly quickly in the open or slowly amongst foliage. Some bats can even hover to pick an insect off foliage.

and at least 50mm (2½in) long, better still the full width of the box. Do not treat the wood with preservatives. As for siting, generally speaking, boxes which face south are used in spring and summer while those which face north are more likely to be used in autumn and winter. The height above ground is apparently not critical, say somewhere between 2 and 5m (7–16ft), but make sure there is a clear flight path to the landing, free of crowding branches and, if possible, shelter from prevailing winds.

If it is adopted, your bat box may offer a temporary home for anything up to fifty bats. As with birds, the bat boxes are most likely to be used in places where there is a shortage of natural roost sites. It is easy to tell if they have been occupied, for there will be the characteristic blackish-brownish droppings.

If your box isn't adopted within a few years, move it and try again. If birds are perverse enough to find their way in, grin and bear it, clearing the nest away in autumn. But bear in mind that it has been known for both bats and birds to cohabit peacefully.

Plenty of night-flying moths end up as an owl's hors d'oeuvres. But the bat is a greater moth-hunter, the only true flying mammal and as well equipped in his way for insect-catching as the owl. And, like an owl, a bat has a velvety coat, only of course his is fur instead of feather. Bats rely mainly on sound to find their way about. Their eyes are small, but they can see well enough: 'Blind as a bat' is yet another unscientific and inaccurate bit of name-calling! They wake up early enough in the evening to take full advantage of the light and the later diurnal-flying insects. Go out as dusk falls and you will usually see a bat of some sort hawking about, putting on a sudden spurt as it homes in on its prey. As it gets darker, cockchafers and moths are snapped up and the real work starts.

The darker it gets, the more the bat relies on its superb sound system, a sophisticated echo-location unit whereby it hears the world instead of seeing it. While we 'watch where we go' in avoiding obstacles, the bat 'listens where he goes' and avoids them just as effectively. Bats are entirely useful beasts to welcome to your garden. They eat nothing but insects. So do your bit to dispel the prejudice and ignorance that surrounds them, build a bat box, enjoy watching them flitting about in the warm summer evenings, and feel privileged if they roost in your attic!

Squirrels

Not all the nests that decorate your garden belong to birds. If you have trees, or if you adjoin a park or cemetery or some such place with a fair sprinkling of trees, you will have squirrels, and they build their substantial dreys in trees. Like birds, they choose to live near you mainly because of the available food, but obviously they must have a suitable nest-site.

Red squirrels are the most popular with their long bushy tails and conspicuous ear tufts, but they are much less widespread than the ubiquitous grey. With a marked preference for conifer woods, red squirrels are subject to population fluctuations, which result in periodic scarcity, so you are lucky if you have them. Just precisely what the factor is that favours the grey squirrel is not clear, but it is true that in the long term the red does not do well in areas where the grey species is abundant. Red squirrels do not fight with the greys, any more than they do amongst themselves. The red squirrel was already declining in numbers before the grey was so ill-advisedly introduced, back at the end of the 19th century. It was in London and at Woburn Abbey that the first grey squirrels, imported from North America, were released and in no time at all this adaptable opportunist was well established. At first it was regarded entirely as a charmer, but it was not long before its bad habits upset the foresters. Eating new shoots and ring-barking trees, the grey squirrel quickly became a severe pest. Quite apart from their tree damaging activities, grey squirrels have a well-developed taste for eggs, young birds and young green shoots of all kinds, not to mention peanuts.

Grey squirrels have a regrettable interest in titboxes.

The red squirrel drey is a compact and substantial ball of twigs and bark, lined with grasses and leaves, placed where a branch joins the main trunk of a tree. The grey's drey is rather more domed, and may be out from the trunk, placed in a large fork.

Grey squirrels will eat almost anything. The red is particularly fond of pine cones, which it will collect off the ground and take to a safe branch where it eats away at the seeds, flicking the scales away until the finished cone is thrown away looking rather like an apple core.

Foxes

Foxes 'go to earth' in a surprising variety of locations. They may take over a rabbit burrow or share a badger sett, find a cavity under rocks or squat under your garden shed. Put your face close and take a deep sniff, an occupied fox den will smell acrid, a full-bellied carnivore smell.

Foxes are not uncommon garden residents. Many people don't even know they're there. Many more people know they're there and take pleasure in the knowledge, for the fox is one of those animals for which we have a fellow-feeling. It is always a significant sign when we give an animal a nickname and perhaps we like the somewhat disreputable, cunning nature of the beast. Like us, or rather like something we used to be, Reynard or Old Daddy Fox is a hunter and an opportunist. He takes risks and cocks a snook when the occasion demands it. He is a carnivore and particularly intelligent, with a large brain for his size. He has acute senses; he is fast and cheeky. For all the nonsense written in newspapers whenever there's a hard winter, he is not a pack animal and there is no chance that he will terrorize the neighbourhood. Perhaps this sort of legend stems from a dim memory of the wolf packs which scourged wild country a long time ago (the wolf persisted in Scotland until the 18th century).

Anyway, the fox does well in the suburbs, mostly because people like to see him. He will eat anything, scavenging bird tables and litter bins, even compost heaps. Very often the noise of the dustbin lid being upturned is the first sign that he is about, and many people have had their first view of a fox from the bedroom window. In the days not so long ago when offal was chucked into the streets, our towns were scavenged by crows and kites; today's scavengers are pigeons, herring gulls and foxes, though maybe it won't be long before red kites scavenge our streets again.

Foxes take pigeons and poultry when they get the chance. Many an exotic duck or goose from an ornamental pond ends up feeding a fox family. They have been known to dash out and take food from delivery vans. Possibly they nobble the occasional domestic cat, but there is more talk than evidence.

Foxes commonly set up their home earth under a shed at the bottom of the garden, knowing they're on to a good thing, a ready supply of food and a quiet place to spend the day before coming out at dusk to be watched from the window by the fellow who kindly puts out a tray of food or makes sure the bird table is well stocked. The fox will quickly learn to put in a regular appearance. His bad habits are easily defined and not too awful to be tolerated. He has a powerful smell, the vicinity of the earth is well-marked and he has an untidy tendency to strew old bones and chicken feathers about. All he asks in return is peace and quiet for his daytime sleep in a well-drained and dry place. It doesn't have to be underground – a hole in the wall or a tree trunk or the space under a garden shed will do. If all goes well, he will eventually invite a vixen to shack up with him and there will be half-a-dozen cubs. Then the vixen will stay away all day, but return at dusk with food. She yaps, and out come the cubs to feed and then to play. Foxes and dogs may chase each other happily round and round a house without any malice aforethought. Foxes even play with cats. For the cubs of course, playing is a serious affair. Typical behaviour for carnivores, it is the process of learning to hunt and kill, just as the playful kitten learns to smell and pounce, explores the lie of the land and discovers how to stalk. Foxplay is much more like the world of the cat, rather than the typical puppy play, which mostly involves headlong chase, rip and tear.

   Foxes have been seen playing in the sandy bunkers of the golf club. They even run off with golf balls, later found severely chewed! And they are well established in city parks.

Brock the badger will be pleased to visit nightly for handouts and may even come during the day, when he takes no notice of scolding birds like these long-tailed tits.

Badgers

Foxes have the sense to cause minimal local disturbance apart from a tendency to untidiness, but a badger in the garden is a mixed blessing, however well disposed you might be. The few people I have known who have had badgers on their garden checklist have just had to give in gracefully and give up all thoughts of gardening in the conventional sense. (Though if you want to discourage them, it

On emerging from the sett, the badger will groom vigorously.

is said that you should pour human urine round the edge of your property from a watering can...) The sett is usually, but not invariably, on sloping ground, in hilly country or woodland edge, so if your garden doesn't fit the bill you can relax. But the wood doesn't have to be a big one, and access to a golf course, railway embankment, park or gravel pit may be positive assets for a badger. There will need to be water of some sort nearby, preferably a stream or river. If all the signs are propitious, then the excavating and earthworks begin. The entrance holes are large, and there may be a lot of them. There will be well-trodden paths and play places, and few obstructions will be tolerated. There won't be much mess about, certainly not waste food, but possibly some stray bedding material like bracken and grasses. Over a period of years the whole character of your property will be changed. The landscaping will be on the grand scale, with much displacement of soil by the time Capability Badger has finished work.

The lawn will be explored for earthworms with many scratchings and scrapings, and at a discreet distance from the sett there will be dung pits, small shallow diggings decorated with the badger's offerings – it is a very fastidious animal.

In the country badgers are common partly because they have the good sense to keep a low profile. Although badgers are now protected in law, centuries of persecution and abuse have taught them to keep themselves to themselves in the interests of survival. Plenty of farmers have badger setts under their chicken houses, and no one is any the worse off. Sometimes people don't even know they're there, but in your garden you cannot fail to know about it.

Having said all the bad things, we don't have to look far for the good ones. No trouble during the day, the badger will come out at dusk and put on a display of great appeal. It is a beautiful animal to see, big and woolly. It has an endearing habit of scratching with gay abandon, has playful cubs, and if you put out food, it will come right up to the window to feed by your side. Worms and beetles may be its natural diet, but it will accept chocolate or honey or peanuts with enthusiasm. Have some regard for its teeth, though, for chocolate can't be

Tales of the riverbank

Count yourself lucky if your garden fronts on to a riverbank and you have water voles burrowing into the bank – this little mammal is now so rare that it is given special protection under the Wildlife and Countryside Act – and prosecutions have resulted from disturbing it and destroying its habitat. Water voles may look like rats but they can be easily identified when swimming because their head and back stay clear of the water surface.

too good for it; perhaps minced meat and scraps would be more thoughtful. It will be regular in its habits and will prefer you to be the same. From its point of view you are an acceptable neighbour and provided you keep yourself to yourself it will repay the compliment. It is unlikely to eat the cat, or your bantams, but it might enjoy your beans, so lay a rope soaked in diesel oil around them, for badgers don't like its smell.

Why do they have that striking white head, with the two bold black stripes down through the eye? Probably it is a warning device. Like the diagonal stripes on heavy lorries it means 'I am dangerous, get out of the way'. Badgers, like hedgehogs, hardly bother to avoid drawing attention to themselves: they blunder through the undergrowth like bulldozers. Hedgehogs feel safe underneath all those prickles; maybe badgers feel safe just because they're big and strong, with powerful teeth. They've no need to bother about their prey hearing them coming; most of their prey species wouldn't know what was happening till it was too late, and are too slow to escape anyway. The badger is a forager by nature, very different in character and interests from that other garden beast, the fox.

Rabbits

Rabbits are rarely welcome in a garden, although they make good lawnmowers at first. If they are about you'll see them at dusk and at dawn, nibbling away in a delicate manner. But put some netting around your young trees, for they won't withstand the onslaught of those bark and bud nibblers. And defend your veg patch. As a landscape artist the rabbit is second only to the badger, and for that reason alone can be an uncomfortable neighbour.

'The rabbit has a charming face;
Its private life is a disgrace.
I really dare not name to you,
The awful things that rabbits do.' Anon.

Roe deer are our most widespread native deer. Roses and ornamental shrubs are favourite garden snacks.

Deer

Large mammals such as deer may not be universally welcome in the garden. Of the six species that occur in the British Isles, gardens are likely to be visited by three: muntjac, roe and fallow.

Muntjac

Only about 44cm (18in) high at the shoulder, muntjac can easily be mistaken for a creeping dog, and in fact their other name is 'barking deer' for they have a short dog-like call. Introduced to Bedfordshire in the 19th century, it is now widespread in many parts and surprisingly numerous (current estimates might be as many as two million in Britain).

Roe

Deer fawns may have spawned the Bambi legend, but your real-life flesh-and-blood roe deer will create havoc. Roe are uncomfortable neighbours, but if you want to attract them, they will be grateful for a salt lick, for example, which provides welcome minerals. You may have some success with carrots too and these are certainly worth trying, but even these will only work if conditions are severe, with snow covering their natural food. In Germany, where they endure worse winters than ours, roe are attracted to haybags slung from trees. They can be a real problem in an orchard where they browse the leaves and buds off apple trees, and may even eat the whole tree when it is young. But they are most likely to find their own way into your garden to enjoy your roses, strawberries and ornamental shrubs. Brambles are part of their staple diet, and – unfortunately for gardeners – roses and strawberries are related to blackberries! So create natural woodland conditions in your garden and you may be lucky, especially if you are in the midst of real woodland.

Munching muntjac

Delicate hoofmarks may be the only clue as to what has been eating your favourite plants. Muntjac might be very small and secretive, but they have a voracious appetite that includes many plants, even yew and rhododendron, that other creatures avoid. However, if your roses get dead-headed before their time, suspect roe deer.

Fallow

Fallow deer are natives of southern Europe and Asia Minor, though they lived in Britain during the last interglacial period. They were reintroduced to Britain, probably by the Normans. They were highly regarded both for their meat and for the hunting sport they offered and as the years went by many enclosures – deer parks – were constructed to provide exclusive and easy hunting for landowners. By the early 17th century every English gentleman of standing had a substantial area of park surrounded by a high wall or a ha-ha which was designed to keep the deer within bounds. In law, ownership of park deer has always depended on their being inside the fence. If they wandered outside, they then belonged to the person whose land they trod (and any damage they caused was his problem). Inevitably, through the years, either by luck or exceptional skill or because the walls had been breached, deer found their way out of the enclosures. So a well-conducted park not only kept its fences in good repair but provided a one-way ramp which allowed deer from outside to find their way inside with ease.

Fallow are at their most wary during the day, as most deer are, and show themselves mostly at dawn and dusk. It is not difficult to encourage them to a feeding station. They may well come to your garden to enjoy your fruit, or you may prefer to offer pony or calf-rearing nuts, or maize tails – all will be gratefully received. Keep well out of sight, sound and smell at first, only revealing yourself over a period of weeks, but in the end you could be handfeeding. In time you will have little difficulty in persuading a splendid fallow buck to take a potato or cattle nuts from your hand. Early August is probably the best time. In spring they are preoccupied with antler-casting and in autumn they are even more preoccupied with the rut, a time when they should be left in peace.

Fallow deer keep out of sight near built-up areas during the day-time, lying up in deep vegetation where they can drowse in peace. At dusk they venture out to patronise fields for sweet grasses and woodland for the new foliage of deciduous trees. Acorns and beech mast are important in autumn and winter.

Bugs and slugs

Although it is perhaps only natural that our attention should be drawn at least at first to the larger creatures, the birds and mammals, other animals are equally interesting and entertaining, and often highly beneficial to the garden. Here, we look at just a few of the host of invertebrate creatures and other forms of wildlife that make up our garden communities.

Take insects, for instance. Many people regard all insects as pests whereas, in fact, only a few hundred out of more than 20,000 British species can reasonably be classified as harmful; by harmful, I mean those that interfere with human activities, damage crops and so forth. No doubt the pests themselves would take a different view. Many of the species not only live without encroaching on our lives, but are of great benefit to us. Pollinating bees are an obvious example of how useful insects can be, and a wide variety of flies, beetles, butterflies, moths and wasps also pollinates many flowers. Ladybirds prey on such harmful insects as aphids and thrips, so if you find a winter colony of ladybirds hibernating in some crevice, leave them in peace. Dragonflies are good value, eating many other insect species which we regard as harmful. Above all, spiders work to our benefit, taking a great quantity of insects. A garden without slugs and insects would in fact very soon be chaos. No bug is superfluous and where would the blackbird be without the worm?

Fairy rings and fungi

A favourite hunting ground of the blackbird and several other birds is the lawn. Artificial and man-made though it may be, the green sward of a lawn, clearly observable and yet a constant attraction to bug, beast and bird, is a boon to the naturalist-gardener.

The fly agaric gets its name from its use in medieval times, when it was crushed into dishes of milk to stupefy the flies which came to drink. An easy toadstool to recognize, usually associated in late summer with birch trees.

Most of the weeds that colonize a lawn are not very popular, but some of the species of fungi are at least spectacular. You may be lucky enough to have the field mushroom growing in fairy rings, especially if the lawn is amply fertilized with horse manure. Puff balls are common on lawns and are perfectly edible, though you should remove the skin before cooking. Eat them while they are young and white, long before they reach the exploding stage.

But perhaps the most attractive of lawn fungi is the mushroom *Marasmius orcades*. This is the culprit responsible for those dark and mysterious fairy rings on lawns – marks that remain long after the mushrooms have disappeared. An insubstantial phenomenon, the mushroom is about 5cm (2in) high and a bit wider, with a fragile stem only about 3mm (⅛in) in diameter. Other species produce rings but this one, common in summer and spring, is most likely to surprise your lawn. The performance starts from a central point and grows outwards like the ripples from a stone thrown in a pond, each specimen producing formidable quantities of spores. The mycelium – the underground portion – persists after the overground ripple has passed by; indeed it lasts for many years. As time goes by chemical action in the soil has a fertilizing effect and stimulates the grass to ever more luxuriant growth, again in the ripple form, but as the fungus ring expands, year by year, its filament roots choke the air spaces in the soil. Rain water cannot drain through properly and the grass is deprived at the very time its healthy growth is demanding a good supply of water. The virtual drought kills the grass and soon there is a bare ring (where the fairies dance) inside the still-flourishing and expanding mushroom ring, firmly based on the unseen but vital mycelium. In time, as the mushroom ring expands still further, the inner clogging mycelium dies, the rain penetrates once again and life begins anew for the grass.

Some of the ink-caps emerge in surprising numbers on made-up ground. They may be edible if cooked young, but it's probably best to take no chances. leave them as objects of beauty – nature's garden ornaments.

Bugs in the borders

If the lawn is an open stage presenting public drama, then we must look to the paths, the flower borders and the jungle interior of the shrubbery for the backstage drama. And of the life struggles and pleasures played out here, we shall only catch revealing glimpses. Lift a stone at the edge of the lawn or on a path and a whole new world comes into view. Ants, spiders and bugs scurry away into the nearest patch of darkness. They don't like the sun. They prefer the moist secret place under the protection of that stone. So put the stone back carefully after having a good look.

There are fairies at the bottom of our garden.

Fairies and chimneys Rose Fyleman (1877–1957)

One of the creatures you are most likely to uncover is the woodlouse. This one especially will shun the warmth of the sun. It is a crustacean, closely related to the marine shrimps and lobsters. Most of the Class are aquatic and the woodlouse is one of the very few to adapt, fairly successfully, to life ashore. Unlike spiders and insects it is not watertight, and its lifestyle is heavily geared to the avoidance of desiccation. It is very sensitive to fluctuations in temperature and humidity, and in dry conditions it quickly succumbs. So it looks for a home under a stone or behind the loose bark of a dead tree. And it is most active at night, when the air is damper. The pill woodlouse rolls into a ball when disturbed, rather like a hedgehog.

Spring flowers such as this wood anemone are a vital source of nectar fuel for insects just emerging from their winter hibernation.

I suppose rolling up helps to protect it from small attackers, but not from robins and blackbirds, or hedgehogs for that matter. But most spiders are reluctant to take them, one exception being a beast called *Dysdera,* a red-legged pale-yellow-bodied nocturnal spider.

Ants

Another creature you will find under a stone is the garden black ant. It has to be said that ants can also be found invading the house, pioneering five-lane antways across your carpets on their way to the sugar in the pantry. This is the species involved in those spectacular marriage flights. When disturbed, there is a great panic in the nest, and the workers bustle about, picking up eggs, grubs and cocoons and carrying them below to underground chambers. They live in a world of touch and smell, light just spelling trouble for them. The wingless ants are the Workers, which has to be spelt with a capital W, because they do everything. Divided into groups, there are those which forage for food; nurserymaids, caring for the eggs and larvae, regulating their warmth and humidity by moving them about the nest; workers-in-waiting to the Queen; soldiers on guard, their weapons their acid-squirting tails or their bites. On lifting a stone or piece of bark you only reveal the tip of the iceberg. Underground is a whole series of galleries and nest chambers. The colony is no passing fancy; it is a long-term project, growing all the time. Occasionally there will be a palace revolution and splinter groups will break away to establish themselves elsewhere.

Consider the situation on a sultry day in late summer when the garden ants indulge in spectacular marriage displays. Young males and queens emerge from the comfortable obscurity of the underground nest, accompanied by great numbers of excited workers. While the earthbound workers mill about on the paving stones or the grass, the winged males and queens take to the air for the marriage flight. The impregnated queens then adventure off to found new colonies. The number of insects involved in these flights is prodigious, and as weather conditions are critical the swarms may emerge simultaneously from many gardens in a neighbourhood. Then

When the garden ants emerge on a sultry summer day to indulge in marriage flights, starlings, black-headed gulls and other birds, such as common terns take advantage of a feeding bonanza.

there will be a spirit of carnival abroad, quickened by the prompt arrival of swallows, house martins and swifts taking advantage of the easy pickings. Sad to think of the joyous flight being so rudely disturbed, but the relationships between hunter and hunted need to be looked at coolly.

Ants are regarded as pests by most gardeners, and they can do harm by loosening soil around plant roots. But they are great destroyers of yet other 'pests', emerging from their nests to hunt small insects and caterpillars and to exploit aphids for their 'milk'.

Iron shelter

I think no garden is complete without a sheet of corrugated iron carefully placed to provide a happy home for all sorts of creatures, including field mice and toads and slow worms. Slow worms, especially, are very common in my area, and it is rare indeed in summer time to lift the corrugated sheet without finding at least one. Legless lizards, they much enjoy basking in the sun, but like to retreat to the security of the underworld below a log or stone, or even a pile of leaves.

Glorious weeds

Many flower borders seem to consist of a few carefully planted annuals surrounded by a desert of bare earth, and the bare earth is an abominable sight, non-productive and extremely difficult to maintain.

Shock-headed Dandelion
That drank the fire of the sun.

The Idle Flowers Robert Bridges

Summer visitors, the brilliant red admirals even show up in city gardens. Nettle beds suit them well for egg-laying, and in due course they are fond of windfalls and over-ripe fruit. Don't be too tidy, nature enjoys some mess.

Plants have a powerful urge to grow, and given the warmth and light of the sun you will have a life's work trying to stop them and it is a crime against life to try. Given the sun as our primary source of energy, green plants, by virtue of photosynthesis, are the only agents capable of converting this energy into food suitable for animals. Bare patches of earth make no useful contribution at all. The striking thing about those plants we choose to call weeds is that they are fast movers, with a fierce desire to succeed, in direct contrast to the reluctance of some of those exotic introductions, which decorate many gardens. It's difficult to get on top of a plant like a dandelion which may produce 12,000 seeds, each keen to keep the species going and to make its own mark. Their advantage is that they belong here, and they succeed by virtue of thousands of years of Nature's research and development which has equipped them for this particular niche, without any artificial propagation or marketing skills. Most of our garden activities, like weeding or pest control, seem designed to eliminate or reduce competition and it's an uphill struggle. Lie back and enjoy those dandelions.

Slugs and snails

Slugs and snails are most interesting animals, yet they appeal to few. Slimy crawlers, leaving a trail of snotty mucus behind them, eating your prize plants secretly by dead of night – they can't win. Although it may seem that their principal food is young lettuces, the fact is that there are many species and they are very catholic in their tastes, mostly going for damaged or decomposing vegetable material. Some live underground, some feed mainly on fungi and animal droppings, some climb plants. And of course their depredations are most noticeable in the spring. As for the slime, it is their protective shell. Few predators relish it, so the slug survives. But it presents a problem at mating time, solved as the two partners first line up alongside each other and then eat each other's slime, before exchanging sperm.

Slugs are snails. Both of these creatures are molluscs. But in the slug the shell is as near absent as makes no difference. In biological terms there is little distinction between them, but in human terms most people find the snail the more endearing, or less repulsive, of the two! Certainly the shell is a marvel of engineering, and a most beautiful form when looked at with a modicum of objectivity. While a mammal's interior skeleton is covered with muscles and soft pliable skin, insects and their like have their strengthening material on the outside, rather like a coat of armour. In molluscs like the snail, the cuticle forms this exoskeleton, a fine piece of structural engineering. Cuticle is a strong composite material rather like fibreglass, with the protein chitin as a fibre component. As the snail grows, so the shell grows with it; molluscs do not moult in the style of insects. But a built-in snag limits the physical size of both: as the animal becomes larger the exoskeleton gets relatively thinner, so it is vulnerable to buckling. A mammal skeleton is cushioned from shock. A snail is condemned to being snail-sized, and the giants so popular in science fiction are doomed to stay on the drawing board.

The commonest garden snail is *Helix aspersa*, a sadly treated species for one so perfect. Its colour and shape may vary from region to region, according to the character of the soil and, to a certain extent, the activities of predators. In areas where chalk is scarce its shell will be thinner. It makes its home under a stone, in a wall crevice or under a convenient plank of wood and once chosen, it returns there after every foraging trip. Generations of snails will use a particularly enticing hole, so that in the course of time they enlarge it, especially where the rock is soft, such as limestone. Snails are hermaphrodites, each individual having both male and female sex organs, but they join

Slugs may not appeal to many people, but to the common toad they are delectable delicacies.

together in order to exchange sperm, after an astonishing courtship ceremony in which you may actually see them approach each other and fire chalky darts into each other's skin. The egg masses of miniature ping pong balls are a common sight under stones.

It is hardly necessary to say what snails eat, but it is only fair to point out that they prefer nettles when they're given the option. And remember that snails themselves are good to eat for man and beast. It is the largest British snail, *H. pomatia*, that is most prized for the table. A large creamy-yellow snail, commonest in chalk or limestone downland, it is known as the Roman snail since it is supposed to have been the Romans who introduced it. In fact the Romans are said to have fattened it for the table much as they encouraged pigeon squabs. Anyway, this is the edible 'escargot'. In fact the garden snail *H.aspersa* is also perfectly edible and is doubtless often enough passed off as *pomatia*, in a triumph of commerce over biology.

Many other creatures eat snails, including their arch-enemy the hedgehog, everybody's garden pet. But there are one or two curious techniques used by would-be consumers of meat for dealing with the problem of the shell which protects it. Glow worms, for instance, are fond of snails. These large beetle larvae first paralyse the mollusc by injection; the meat liquefies and the insect sucks it up, leaving an empty shell. The technique of the song thrush, while less horrifying, is scarcely less delicate. Choosing a suitable stone as an anvil, the thrush hops into the flower border to find a specimen of *Cepaea*, the exotically banded and colour-camouflaged hedge snail, carries the

The song thrush beats a snail on an anvil until the shell is broken off. It then wipes the snail free of slime before eating it.

victim to the anvil and smashes the shell into several pieces. Probably it will then wipe the slime off the body, as it does with a slug, before eating it. Now the interesting thing about this activity is that though the snail exists in a whole variety of colour and banding patterns, an individual thrush tends to select

one particular version of the snail. Once it has 'got its eye in' on, say, a pink snail with four black bands, that is the one it invariably goes for. You can confirm this by examining the broken shell pieces around the anvil. (Beware of an anvil used by more than one thrush!) So the thrush acts as an evolutionary agent, encouraging the snail to produce a whole range of cryptic colorations.

And though she doth but very softly go,
However 'tis not fast, nor slow, but sure;
And certainly they that do travel so,
The prize they do aim at, they do procure.

Upon the Snail John Bunyan (1628–1688)

Why is the song thrush the only British bird that does this? There is no structural adaptation – no anatomical suitability – which gives the thrush an edge over other birds and fits him specially for it. Opportunist blackbirds often steal snails from thrushes – indeed they have learnt to listen for the sound of the thrush hammering snails on the anvil, so that they may hasten to enjoy the reward without doing any of the work. But the nearest a blackbird has been seen to engage in snail-bashing for itself is when it has shaken the snail vigorously in a variation of the beak-wiping movement. So we must be left with admiration for the two song thrushes which were once seen to deal with 29 snails in less than eight hours.

Ladybirds

The flower border has many examples of the curious predator/prey relationships. The inoffensive-looking ladybird may not look like a carnivore, but a meat-eating predator it is. Not exactly the cunning fox or the swift sparrowhawk of the insect world, it ambles quietly up to take advantage of the greenfly, which never consider the possibility of running away. So cosy is the relationship that the ladybird beetle lays its eggs conveniently close to a colony of greenfly aphids; when the larvae emerge, the dining room is close by, and they can munch at leisure. And when they are grown into the full brightly coloured glory of adult ladybirds they have the security of being thoroughly distasteful themselves, so that they are relatively immune from attack.

Those bright reds and blacks serve as a warning to allcomers that they are unpalatable. Other, less fortunate, insects must protect themselves by camouflage colouring, or by venturing out only at night, or by living underground.

Bugboxes offer a safe winter haven for the ladybirds which are so helpful in controlling aphids.

Aphids

Ladybirds aren't the only aphid-botherers. Blue tits will eat them, hoverflies and lacewings will eat them, in enormous quantities. But there are enormous quantities to be eaten as the aphids multiply at a rate which makes rabbits look like reluctant beginners. The eggs are laid at the beginning of winter to hatch in March, promptly setting about the task of producing living young, which hatch from eggs incubated inside the parent body. These young mature in ten days and produce more young. These can fly and settle on herbaceous plants to feed and produce more offspring. The generations are flightless and winged alternately, and each flying generation takes itself off to pioneer the technique elsewhere. Each female greenfly produces several offspring every day during her short life, and a single one may be responsible for over 1300 descendants in a fortnight. It is just as well that the blue tits and hoverflies are waiting.

There are many different species of aphid. Some of them – sap-suckers – pierce the tissues of plant shoots and suck with a tube-like mouth. Under a bad infestation the leaves and shoots of the plant may become distorted, in extreme cases killed. Some, like the blackfly, attack broad beans and some, like the rose-greenfly, attack roses, a crime for which they suffer heavily to the benefit of the chemical industry's bank balance. Extracting sustenance from the sap-cells of the rose plant produces a waste product of sugar and water, which is excreted by the aphids. This is keenly enjoyed by other bugs, which encourage the good work. The garden ant, for instance, will perambulate among the aphids, stroking their abdomens with antennae to stimulate the sweet secretion. Then they take the sugar water back to the underground nest for the ant larvae to enjoy.

Aphids are subject to occasional migratory urges, when they abandon roses for grasses or some other food plant. But there are other creatures having business with the rose, which in all conscience has to be a good thing, since of all garden plants the rose is just about the most unproductive of useful food for other garden-livers, as opposed to garden-lovers!

Spiders

In visiting flowers, insects put themselves at risk from birds and other predators. As they travel between the flower heads they run the gauntlet of the spider traps. Spiders catch insects with a wide range of techniques: setting sticky snare-webs of orb, purse, triangular or hammock shape or open trellis work; or jumping, ambushing and chasing without the use of a web at all. The web spiders live in a world of silk and vibrations, the hunting spiders in a world of sight and touch.

'Will you walk into my parlour?' said a spider to a fly:

The Spider and the Fly Mary Howitt

The most common garden spider is the garden cross, the large beast with the striking white cross on its abdomen. It makes its web soon after dark, when you can watch it perform very easily with the discreet use of a torch. The main frame is a permanent structure, but every night it erects new radial threads, then spirals outwards from the centre. With a stable structure complete, it spins a second spiralling, this time using a different silk, gum coated. The spinning is done with the spinnerets, three pairs of appendages on the abdomen. Rather like fingers, at their tips are dozens of minute spinning tubes that extrude fluid silk; this hardens on contact with air.

Long-tailed tits relish spiders, and the web wouldn't have lasted long anyway.

Different internal glands produce different qualities of silk – main grid, radii, spiral and sticky spiral.

When an insect is stuck fast, its struggles transmit vibrations along the 'telegraph cable' to the spider safely hidden under a leaf. The spider then emerges to use its senses of sight and smell to evaluate the position. (If a leaf has blown into the trap by mistake, the spider cuts it out and releases it.) A suitable insect is bitten and injected with poison, then wrapped in a silken shroud drawn from the spinnerets by the hind legs. If the insect is big or difficult to handle, it may be made immobile by binding with silk before the injection. In order to suck the goodness from the prey, the spider injects it with fluid that liquefies the tissues, for its small mouth cannot deal with solid food. It can go for a long time without eating, but needs water, which is why you so often find house spiders in the basin or the bath.

In the late autumn the garden cross spider spins a cocoon of yellow silk in which she lays several hundred eggs. Hidden under bark or an overlapping plank on an outhouse or somewhere similar, they will sit out the winter to hatch in spring. Why are we all so frightened of spiders? Because they are hairy, and because they have long skinny legs and fast unpredictable movements. They live secret lives in dark crannies, trap their prey by unsportsmanlike methods and eat them in bizarre circumstances. On top of all that, some of them can bite and they're bites are poisonous, although fortunately in the British Isles, only mildly so. And yet, like most other predators, spiders are themselves sought by many hungry eyes. Toads like them, and so do hunting wasps. And birds are death to spiders. Wrens, especially, birds of the hedgeways and crannies, are great spider collectors.

A red-tailed bumble bee on lesser celandine.

Bees

Honey Bees

Honey bees may nest in tree holes, the sort of places attractive to tits. Blue tits will deliberately hang about the hive entrance (this applies to the man-made beehive as well) picking off the odd bee. In fact in some parts of

Bee boles were recesses built into a wall to house the straw skeps that served as bee hives.

the country they are actually known as bee birds, along with the whitethroat and the spotted flycatcher, all keen bee-fanciers. Both bees and wasps are good to eat, except for the sting of course, and the tits know the difference between the male (stingless) bee and the female stingers, and deal with them accordingly. Blue tits may appear to be little charmers, but just see one perching on a branch, holding a bee in one foot and picking at it like a hawk. It is a ferocious little animal. It deals with the venom by beating the bee against the perch, and by rubbing the insect to squeeze out the poison and discard the sting. On a cold day, when bees are torpid, the tits may actually enter the hive to go hunting. They are fond of honey too. Put some on the bird table and you will find it is welcome to tits and also to blackbirds and woodpeckers.

Before sugar, honey was man's only sweetening substance and it is an excellent source of instant energy: one spoonful represents the distillation of nectar from visits to 50,000 flowers. Having found a good source of nectar, the foraging bee returns to the hive and conveys the information to the other bees by dancing. Using the sun as a reference point, his waggle-dance communicates 'bearing and distance-off' and the degree of attractiveness. Bees are principal pollinators of apples, and many fruit growers hire occupied beehives to ensure maximum pollination in their orchards. The bee–human relationship is long established, maybe 10,000 years old, with humans providing a welcome and a house and the bee making honey. Apart from our share of the honey, we benefited from the beeswax, used in the manufacture of things like candles and furniture polish.

Years ago, bees were kept in straw skeps, mostly on benches in the open, or on a shelf in an open-fronted shelter. But in wet and windy areas, beekeepers provided specially designed 'bee boles', recesses built into a wall to house skeps. Mostly they were oriented south or south-east, so that the bees benefited from the morning sun. A honey-bee swarm may contain up to 50,000 individuals at the height of summer.

If you know of any bee bole that may not have been recorded, tell the Dry Stone Walling Asssociation, Milnthorpe, Cumbria LA7 7NH www.dswa.org.uk

Bumble bees are highly desirable garden creatures and they welcome help with nest sites. Put a disused fieldmouse nest-ball (or maybe a moss-ball) under a plant pot, leaving room for the bee to find a way in.

Bumble bees

While birds sample bees in a fairly sophisticated manner, the badger simply excavates a sample of soil, extracting all the worms and grubs he can find. He is particularly fond of a bee's nest. Bumble bees commonly nest under grass or moss and the marauding badger will eat bees, grubs, cocoons, wax, honey and pollen – the lot. Bumble bees like to nest in a field mouse's disused nest-ball; they don't burrow themselves. After hibernation, the queen greets spring by collecting pollen and packing it into a waxy cell into which she lays her eggs. These hatch into grubs, eat the pollen, pupate and hatch into worker bees. The colony reaches its peak in midsummer and in autumn all die except for a few young queens, which hibernate to renew the process the following spring. It is fairly easy to encourage bumble bees to take up residence in much the same way that tits will take to nestboxes. Find an old mouse nest (from under a corrugated iron sheet cunningly left on the ground in a suitable corner for instance) and bury it at ground level under a stone or roof tile to keep the ground dry. Proof the construction against a mouse take-over by covering with half-inch wire netting.

Mining bees

Mining bees are mostly solitary creatures looking much like small honey bees. They burrow and make a little clay pot for the egg cell, stocking it with honey and then putting a lid on it for safety. Sometimes the nest hole will be in a window frame or a ventilation brick or a post; sometimes even a keyhole is pressed into service. The bees may make nest cells in sand or earth in lawns, and one species, *Andrena amata*, makes a little conical pile of earth to mark the entrance. The tunnel may be a around 60cm (2ft) long, filled from the bottom with a line of nest cells containing eggs and the ready supply of instant grub-growth, pollen. The whole process is over and done with by the end of June and, on the credit side, mining bees are most useful as fruit tree pollinators. There are various artificial nestbox designs that serve to attract bees (see page 180).

Several wild plants are especially attractive to bees: viper's bugloss, comfrey, red clover and foxglove are all worth encouraging.

Wasps

As with bees, there are several different kinds of wasps. Social or paper wasps build under eaves, or hanging from an internal joist. At first the nest is the size of a golf ball, beautifully constructed by the queen of papier-mâché made from wood fibre. The first generation of workers is born here, fed and nurtured by the queen on a diet of chewed flies. Extension work to the building makes room for more cells and more workers, and by the time it's finished the nest is the size of a football. At the approach of autumn a generation of males and females is produced with the capacity to fly and mate. The resulting queens hibernate, to survive into the New Year to begin a new colony, while the males die when the cold weather overtakes them.

The docile hornet sometimes nests in outhouses, to the panic of everyone in sight, although it is markedly reluctant to sting. It is much bigger than the common wasp, and is yellow and red instead of yellow and black. Wasps are widely regarded as a nuisance, and countless nests and queens are destroyed; yet arguably they do more good than harm. The worker wasps lead an exemplary life carrying home insect prey to feed their young, and in truth the sting rarely justifies the fear it rouses. Honeybee stings are a great deal worse! Wasp nests are attacked by woodpeckers and by magpies, which rip them apart to extract the pupae and larvae. But sometimes the wasps fight back, and will drive blue tits away from a bone or fruit on the bird table.

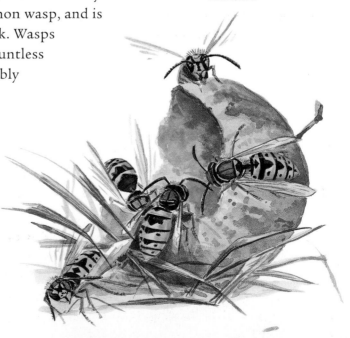

Worker wasps enjoying ripe fruit. They can be tiresome at a picnic but are not intent on stinging, merely seeking high energy food from your delicious jam sandwich. Try not to flap. Remember wasps are at the top of their food pyramid and are effective insect controllers.

Appendices

Taxonomy, or 'What's in a name?'

Putting a name to a bird is arguably the first requirement in getting to know something about it. And a knowledge of bird topography is an important foundation in the building up of identification expertise.

Blue tit to some, tomtit to others and pimplemees to a Dutchman, but *Parus caeruleus* all over the world. The value of scientific names is that being based on a dead language – Latin – they are not subject to the sort of changes brought about by time and common usage, which gives words different meanings in different decades. The value of an ossified language is beyond price to the taxonomist, who catalogues living creatures.

Scientists and philosophers struggled for centuries to devise a practical filing system for classifying the natural world. It was in 1735 that the Swedish naturalist Linnaeus published his watershed work *Systema Naturae*, which established the biological principles for listing plants and animals. He listed into ever smaller groupings those plants or animals which displayed similarities with each other.

Working from the top, he proposed plant and animal Kingdoms. Then, he divided the animals (everything from elephants to sandhoppers) into Phyla, one of which encompasses the vertebrates (animals with backbones). This Phylum, Chordata, as it is known, is further divided into a number of Classes, one of which is for mammals, where we ourselves are placed, another of which is for birds, the Class of Aves. Twenty-six Orders of birds yet again sub-divide into Families, and within the Families a group of closely related birds with common traits of behaviour or plumage or structure represent a Genus, which is finally divided into Species, the 'kinds' of bird.

In this way, a bird is known by its generic name suffixed by its specific name. The blue tit, *Parus caeruleus*, for example, belongs to the tit Family (Paridae) which is part of the perching bird Order of the bird Class of the vertebrate branch of the Animal Kingdom. So, a blue tit from root to blossom:

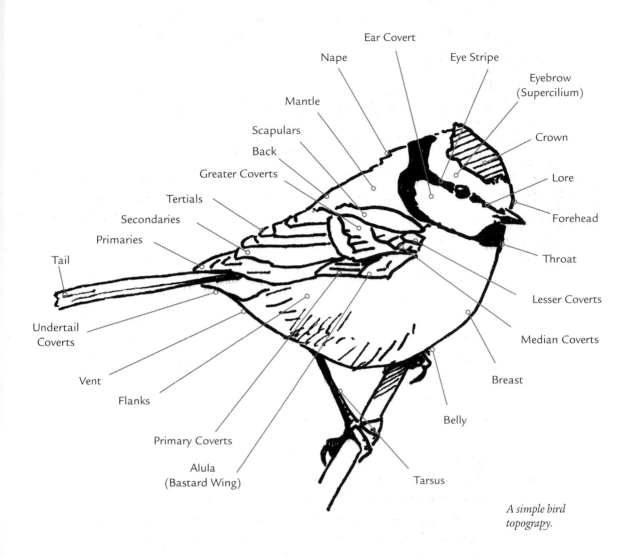

A simple bird topograpy.

Kingdom ANIMALIA
Phylum CHORDATA
Class AVES
Order PASSERIFORMES
Family PARIDAE
Genus PARUS
Species *Parus caeruleus*

There are further divisions into subphyla, sub and super families, and subspecies, but the binomial system which gives most species a name comprising two words seems quite enough to be going on with ...

Tools of the trade

Birdwatching is a modified form of hunting. Primitive hunters sought only to fill their bellies, but if we are to enjoy success in our terms we must use their techniques in our aim of getting close to the quarry, both in the literal sense and in that of getting to know them better. To this day the hunter can teach any aspiring birdman a great deal. Fieldcraft involves a great deal more than wearing a battledress jacket. The hunter knows his prey as well as he is able, he moves quietly and with due regard to the wind and the light, above all he knows time and place. Present-day wildlife photographers face all the problems of the hunter, and it is axiomatic that the best ones are those to whom a knowledge of natural history comes first, before knowledge of film stocks and photo apparatus.

The tools of the trade are important. Keen eyesight and hearing are the naturalist's most precious assets, followed by an ability to use them effectively. Binoculars are well-nigh indispensable, and they are a source of great heart-searching to many would-be birders. The problem is that, like birds, they come in a bewildering variety of guises. To meet all eventualities, you need to own half-a-dozen pairs. However, given that you are to start by buying one pair, you should go for glasses that are reasonably light in weight and which give a bright picture over a medium field of view, with a magnification of 8, 9 or 10 times and objective lenses between 30mm and 50mm in diameter. Thus your chosen binoculars might be described as 8×30 or 10×42, both highly suitable everyday combinations.

Sharp eyes and patient field craft will enable you to seek out birds like this marsh tit rummaging amongst leaf litter.

Whether your interest is in far-flung ornithological expeditions or in studying the action nowhere more demanding than your back garden through the kitchen window with a mug of coffee in your hand, you need to be able to make a positive identification of the birds you see or hear. *Identifying British Birds* by Dominic Couzens, is a useful tool, showing similar species together on the same pages as well as revealing the difference between the sexes and the juveniles and other information. There are a number of field guides to more far-flung identification – hunter's manuals. *Collins Bird Guide* is one of the best, covering the whole of Europe. *The Hamlyn Guide to the Birds of Britain and Europe* by Bertel Bruun, has the great advantage of a conventional layout which marries text, maps and illustrations so that they appear on the same page for each bird.

The chiffchaff's song is very easy to learn (it sings its own name), but for most bird song a CD is a useful learning tool.

You will also need a more general work of background information species by species, and this is well catered for by Jonathan Elphick's succinct *The Birdwatchers Handbook*. And you will want to keep informed with the magazine *Bird Watching*, a lively and authoritative monthly (address page 181).

Books are notoriously poor at imparting information about the sounds made by birds. Yet their calls and songs are often a vital clue to their identification, to say nothing of their state of mind. Probably the best way to learn the birdsong is by way of a knowledgeable companion. But a good record or tape will help. The National Sound Archive's Wildlife section have issued *British Bird Sounds*, which records 175 species on two CDs. The CD-ROM/DVD-ROM interactive guide to British Birds, published by BirdGuides, is expensive but highly recommended, with songs and calls from more than 300 species (available from the RSPB or Jacobi Jayne, see pages 178 and 180). For a useful CD with the songs and calls of common garden birds, try *Garden Bird Songs and Calls* by Geoff Sample.

Bird organizations

The Royal Society for the Protection of Birds (RSPB) The Lodge, Sandy, Bedfordshire SG19 2DL.

Britain's leading conservation organization. This society, first formed in 1889 and now with the strength of well over a million members and managing 150 reserves, must take a place of honour among the many organizations that work on behalf of wildlife. The RSPB has research scientists, wardens, and other specialists – full-time staff earning their living with birds – but its great achievement has been to put the wider importance of the subject across to the general public with enthusiasm through publications, films and meetings. Membership of the RSPB not only gives your soul the warm glow of satisfaction induced by the knowledge that you are making a highly practical contribution to the well-being of all birds, but brings you a number of benefits, not least of which is the excellent quarterly magazine *Birds*. Local groups, run by the RSPB, provide opportunities to join field excursions, to hear top-class speakers and to see the best of the bird films.

The RSPB manages a countrywide network of bird reserves, organizes many exhibitions and meetings, is much concerned with the politics of conservation. All birders should support this admirable and effective society. Write for sales catalogue and membership information. Website: www.rspb.org.uk

(The RSPB relies heavily on the support of volunteers, but you may also want to join your local Naturalists' Trust or Bird Society. There you'll find out what is going on in the area and meet people who will know all about the national bird organizations. Through them your hobby can be harnessed for valuable and exciting research).

RSPB Wildlife Explorers Junior section of the RSPB, for under-19s. 500 groups run by 1,500 volunteers. Projects, holidays, roadshows, competitions and local events. Three magazines aimed at different age groups. Address as RSPB.

The British Trust for Ornithology (BTO) The National Centre for Ornithology, The Nunnery, Thetford, Norfolk IP24 2PU.

The BTO is the major organization which initiates and co-ordinates the sort of research that involves the efforts of a network of birdwatchers covering the whole of Britain. It promotes and encourages the wider understanding, appreciation and conservation of birds through scientific study using the combined skills and enthusiasm of its members, other birdwatchers and its staff. If you want to become actively concerned with census or ringing work, then you need to become a member. The standards are high, the BTO operates to serious scientific criteria, but the range of work is wide enough to encompass everyone from the conscientious beginner to the dedicated professional. The work tends to consist of some form of census – statistical recording of numbers breeding, passing by and wintering – or ringing. The Trust organizes long-running surveys, including the National Ringing Scheme, Nest Record Scheme, Breeding Bird Survey and Waterways Bird Survey. It also runs the Garden Birdwatch scheme, monitoring the importance of the garden habitat. If you'd like to contribute, write for a free information pack (Garden Birdwatch, Freepost, Thetford IP24 2BR). And there is no doubt that this work is invaluable, for birds and bird numbers are among the most sensitive indicators of the health of our environment. Monitoring fluctuations in their numbers provides essential information to those whose job it is to formulate policy in wildlife conservation. At the same time keeping a record of your bird observations will give you immense interest and satisfaction.

Results of these co-operative surveys are communicated to government departments to good effect. The Trust publishes *BTO News* six times a year. All serious birders should join. Write for catalogue and information. Email: info@bto.org Website: www.bto.org

Other wildlife organizations

Barn Owl Trust
Waterleat, Ashburton,
Devon TQ13 7HU
info@barnowltrust.org.uk
www.barnowltrust.org.uk
*Aims to conserve the owl and
encourage education and
information.*

Bat Conservation Trust
Unit 2, 15 Cloisters House,
8 Battersea Park Road,
London SW8 4BG
Tel: 020 7627 2629
Helpline Tel: 0845 1300 228
enquiries@bats.org.uk
www.bats.org.uk

British Deer Society
Fordingbridge,
Hampshire SP6 1EF
Tel: 01425 655434
h.q@bds.org.uk
www.bds.org.uk

British Dragonfly Society
www.dragonflysoc.org.uk

**British Hedgehog
Preservation Society**
Hedgehog House, Dhustone,
Ludlow, Shropshire, SY8 3PL
Tel: 01584 890801

Butterfly Conservation
www.butterfly-conservation.org

**County Naturalists Trusts
and Bird Societies**
*Addresses are usually available
at your local public library.*

**Countryside Council
for Wales**
Maed-y-Ffynnon,
Penrhosgarnedd, Bangor,
Gwynedd LL57 2DW
www.ccw.gov.uk

English Nature
Northminster House,
Peterborough PE1 1UA.
Tel: 01733 455100,
enquiries@English-nature.org.uk
www.English-nature.org.uk
*Useful series of leaflets on garden
subjects, including ponds,
allotments, bats, dragonflies, birds.*

Game Conservancy Trust
Fordingbridge,
Hampshire SP6 1EF
Tel: 01425 652381
www.gct.org.uk

Garden Organic
Ryton Organic Gardens,
Coventry, Warks CV8 3LG.
Tel: 024 7630 3517
enquiry@hdra.org.uk
www.gardenorganic.org.uk
*Researches and promotes organic
gardening. Write for catalogue.*

Hawk and Owl Trust
PO Box 100,
Taunton TA4 2WX
Tel: 0870 990 3889
enquiries@hawkandowl.org
www.hawkandowl.org

Mammal Society
2B Inworth Street,
London SW11 3EP
Tel: 020 7359 2299
www.abdn.ac.uk/mammal

**Northern Ireland
Ornithologists Club**
www.nioc.fsnet.co.uk
*Operates reserves and runs
regular field trips.*

Royal Horticultural Society
80 Vincent Square,
London SW1A 2PE
Tel: 020 7884 4333
info@rhs.org.uk
www.rhs.org.uk

**Royal Pigeon Racing
Association**
The Reddings,
Cheltenham GL51 6RN
Tel: 01452 713529
www.rpra.org

**Royal Society for the
Prevention of Cruelty
to Animals**
Wilberforce Way, Southwater,
Horsham, Sussex RH13 9RS
Tel: 0870 3335 998
www.rspca.org.uk

Scottish Natural Heritage
Rogers Crofts,
12 Hope Terrace,
Edinburgh EH9 2AS
Tel: 0131 446 4784
www.snh.org.uk

Scottish Ornithologists Club
Waterston House, Aberlady,
East Lothian EH32 OPY
mail@the-soc.org.uk
www.the-soc.org.uk

**Universities Federation for
Animal Welfare**
The Old School, Brewhouse
Hill, Wheathampstead,
Hertfordshire AL4 8AN.
www.ufaw.org.uk

Wildfowl and Wetlands Trust
Slimbridge, Glos GL2 7BT
enquiries@wwt.org.uk
www.wwt.org.uk
*Illustrated annual report and
periodical bulletins. Maintains
unique collection of swans, ducks
and geese from all parts of the
world. Reserves, lecture
programme, etc.*

Worldwide Fund for Nature
WWF-UK, Panda House,
Weyside Park, Godalming,
Surrey GU7 1XR
www.wwf.org.uk

Useful names and addresses

*Suppliers of wild bird food
and bird furniture*

Jacobi Jayne & Co.
Wealden Forest Park,
Canterbury, Kent CT6 7LQ
Tel: 0800 072 0130
enquiries@jacobijayne.com
www.jacobijayne.com
www.birdon.com
www.wildbirdnews.com
*First-class selection of the most
effective feeders and nestboxes,
plus much else and the highest
quality wildlife foods. Write for
Wild Bird News, their excellent
free catalogue.*

CJ Wildbird Foods
The Rea, Upton Magna,
Shrewsbury SY4 4UR
Tel: 0800 731 2820
advice@birdfood.co.uk
www.birdfood.co.uk
*Complete RSPB BirdCare range
and collection of wildlife-related
products. First-class catalogue.*

John E Haith Ltd
65 Park Street, Cleethorpes,
North-East Lincolnshire
DN35 7NF
Tel: 0800 298 7054
www.haiths.com
Bird food, feeders and nestboxes.

Wiggly Wigglers,
Lower Blakemere Farm,
Blakemere, Hereford HR2 9PX
www.wigglywigglers.co.uk
for worms

Pond plant suppliers

Anglo Aquarium
Tel: 020 8363 8548
(phone for catalogue)
*Any reputable garden centre
will sell aquatic plants.*

Further reading

General garden and bird books

Baines, Chris 2000 *How to Make a Wildlife
Garden* Elm Tree Books

Bardsley, Louise *The Wildlife Pond Handbook*
The Wildlife Trusts

Bruun, Bertel 2000 *The Hamlyn Guide to
the Birds of Britain and Europe* Hamlyn

Burton, Robert 1991 *The New RSPB
Birdfeeder Handbook* Dorling Kindersley

Burton, Robert 2005 *Garden Bird Behaviour*
New Holland

Burton, Robert 2005 *The Ultimate Birdfeeder
Handbook* New Holland

Cocker, Mark 2005 *Birds Britannica* Chatto
& Windus

Couzens, Dominic 2004 *The Secret Lives
of Garden Birds* Christopher Helm

Couzens, Dominic 2005 *Identifying British
Birds* Collins

du Feu, Chris 2003 *The BTO Nestbox Guide*
BTO

Elphick, Jonathan 2001 *The Birdwatcher's
Handbook* BBC Books

Holden, Peter 2002 *RSPB Handbook
of British Birds* Christopher Helm

Hume, Rob 2002 *RSPB Complete Birds
of Britain and Europe* Dorling Kindersley

Mead, Chris 2000 *The State of the Nation's
Birds* Whittet Books

Moss, Stephen 2003 *The Garden Bird
Handbook* New Holland

Moss, Stephen 2004 *The Bird-Friendly
Garden* Harper Collins

Oddie, Bill 2002 *Bill Oddie's Guide to
Birdwatching* New Holland

Porter, Valerie 1989 *The Pond Book* Croom
Helm

Street, Michael 1994 *(Large) Ponds and Lakes
for Wildlife* Game Conservancy Trust

Svensson, Lars, Mullarney, Killian,
Zetterstrom, Dan and Grant, Peter J 2001
Collins Bird Guide Harper Collins

Toms, Mike 2004 *The BTO GardenWatch
Handbook* British Trust for Ornithology

Wallace, Ian 2004 *Beguiled by Birds*
Christopher Helm

Species studies

An excellent series of pocket guides, including *The Red Mason Bee, Bumblebees, Ladybirds, Spiders, Earthworms* and *Garden Beetles* is available from CJ Wildbird Foods (see opposite). *Hedgehogs and the Gardener* is very useful, published by the Henry Doubleday Research Association (now Garden Organic).

Altringham, John 1998 *Bats: Biology and Behaviour* OUP

Armstrong, Edward A 1992 *The Wren* Shire

Beebee, Trevor 1985 *Frogs & Toads* Whittet

Birkhead, Tim 1991 *The Ecology of Magpies* T & AD Poyser

Boag, David 1988 *The Kingfisher* Blandford

Carter, Ian 2001 *The Red Kite* Arlequin Press

Chinery, Michael 1993 *Spiders* Whittet

Clark, Michael 1988 *Badgers* Whittet

Coombs, Franklin 1978 *Crows* Batsford

Fair, John 1986 *The Mute Swan* Croom Helm

Feare, Chris 1984 *The Starling* Oxford University Press

Goodwin, Derek 1986 *Crows of the World* Natural History Museum, London

Hamilton James, Charlie 1997 *Kingfishers* Colin Baxter

Harris, Stephen 1986 *Urban Foxes* Whittet

Holm, Jessica 1994 *Squirrels* Whittet

Howard, H Eliot 1940 *A Waterhen's Worlds* Cambridge University Press

Kear, Janet 1990 *Man & Wildfowl* T & AD Poyser

Lack, David 1956 *Swifts in a Tower* Methuen

Lack, David 1985 *The Life of the Robin* Witherby

Longbein, Jochen 2004 *Fallow Deer* Mammal Society

Lundberg, Arne 1992 *The Pied Flycatcher* T & AD Poyser

Madge, Steven & Burn, Hilary 1999 *Crows & Jays* Christopher Helm

Matthysen, Erik 1998 *The Nuthatches* T & AD Poyser

Mead, Chris 1984 *Robins* Whittet

Morris, Pat 1983 *Hedgehogs* Whittet

Newton, Ian 1972 *Finches* Collins

Perrins, Chris 1979 *British Tits* Collins

Powell, Dan 1999 *A Guide to the Dragonflies of Great Britain* Arelquin Press

Ratcliffe, Derek 1993 *The Peregrine Falcon* T & AD Poyser

Richardson, Phil 2000 *Bats* Whittet

Roberts, MDL 2000 *Pigeons, Doves and Dovecotes* Golden Cockerel

Sielmann, Heinz 1959 *My Year with the Woodpeckers* Barrie & Rockliff

Simms, Eric 1978 *British Thrushes* Collins

Snow, Barbara and David 1988 *Birds and Berries* T & AD Poyser

Snow, DW 1988 *A Study of Blackbirds* Natural History Museum, London

Summers-smith, JD 1992 *In Search of Sparrows* T & AD Poyser

Tubbs, Colin 1974 *The Buzzard* David & Charles

Turner, Angela 1990 *Swallows and Martins* Croom Helm

Magazines and book suppliers

Bird Watching. An up-to-the-minute monthly magazine, full of practical advice and news, available from news stands or subscription from Bretton Court, Bretton, Peterborough PE3 8DZ Tel: 0870 062 0200 www.greatmagazines.co.uk

BBC Wildlife Magazine. Popular and scientifically accurate articles about wildlife and conservation, often linked to TV and radio programmes. Topical environmental news stories. Origin Publishing Ltd., 14th Floor, Tower House, Fairfax Street, Bristol BS1 3BN wildlifemagazine@originpublishing.co.uk www.bbcwildlifemagazine.com

Natural History Book Service, 2–3 Wills Road, Totnes, Devon TQ9 5XN. Holds the most comprehensive stock of world-wide books and issues an invaluable seasonal catalogue. www.nhbs.com

Index

For the size of their bodies, wrens have an operatic voice. They need a dramatic song-post. They also like to sing into the wind.